GOD *of*
LOVE

A Guide to the Heart of Judaism, Christianity, and Islam

MIRABAI STARR

Monkfish Book Publishing Company
Rhinebeck, New York

God of Love © 2012 by Mirabai Starr

Printed in the United States of America

Library of Congress Cataloging-in-Publication Data

Starr, Mirabai.

God of love : a guide to the heart of Judaism, Christianity, and Islam / Mirabai Starr.

p. cm.

Includes bibliographical references and index.

ISBN 978-0-9833589-2-3 (pbk. : alk. paper)

1. Christianity and other religions. 2. Religions—Relations. 3. Abrahamic religions. I. Title.

BR127.S777 2012

200—dc23

2011050078

"Odes of Solomon" excerpted from *The Enlightened Heart: An Anthology of Sacred Poetry,* copyright (c) 1989 by Stephen Mitchell. Reprinted by permission of HarperCollins Publishers.

Monkfish Book Publishing Company
22 E. Market St., Suite 304 Rhinebeck, New York 12572

For Maharaj-ji, my beloved Baba,
who teaches us that
All is One.

CONTENTS

INTRODUCTION
The Interspiritual Quest

All those who love you are beautiful;
they overflow with your presence
so that they can do nothing but good.
There is infinite space in your garden;
all men, all women are welcome here;
all they need do is enter.

The Odes and Psalms of Solomon

God is love, and those who abide in love abide in God,
And God abides in them.

1 John 4:16

O Marvel! a garden amidst the flames.
My heart has become capable of every form:
it is a pasture for gazelles and a convent for Christian monks,
and a temple for idols and the pilgrim's Ka'ba,
and the tables of the Torah and the book of the Quran.
I follow the religion of Love: whatever way Love's camel takes,
that is my religion and my faith.

Ibn 'Arabi , "O Marvel"

I profess the religion of love,

Love is my religion and my faith.

My mother is love

My father is love

My prophet is love

My God is love

I am a child of love

I have come only to speak of love.

Mevlana Jalaluddin Rumi, "I Profess the Religion of Love"

EVER SINCE I was a little girl, I have been drawn to the living heart of every spiritual tradition I have encountered. Like a night wanderer who comes across a sanctuary in the woods, I peer through the stained-glass window, aching to enter and bow down at the altar I see blazing within.

My eye catches the eye of the man or woman who keeps the fire there, a person properly attired in the vestments of their creed. We smile and nod to one another in wordless agreement: their task is to tend that hearth; mine to move on, map the terrain, marking each resting place and blessing the wilderness between.

This powerful attraction to religion makes no sense. In fact, for much of my life it embarrassed me. I grew up in a secular Jewish family, in which my parents made a compelling case for renouncing organized religion on the grounds that religious institutions have been responsible for the most horrendous violations of human rights— and of the planet herself—in the history of so-called civilization. Their indictment was especially aimed at the

Judeo-Christian traditions and their glorification of an abusive Father-God who is forever punishing His children in fits of divine fury.

As I began to study and practice Eastern spiritual traditions with Western-born teachers—refugees from their own Jewish and Christian backgrounds—I found the God of my ancestors being similarly dismissed. Yet these same spiritual guides could not seem to resist the impulse to winnow the Testaments, Old and New, and emerge with vibrant wisdom teachings that transcend dogma and make their way directly to the heart. My Buddhist and Hindu teachers wove these shining Western threads into their talks and books.

In solidarity with my nontheistic family, I tried to cultivate a general attitude of condemnation toward all religious institutions for being naïve, patriarchal, and potentially dangerous. Yet, a single line from the Song of Songs, the Gospel of John, or the poetry of Rumi would make my heart fly open and soar, arcing toward a God I could not bring myself to believe in. What I found irresistible was the essential unity at the core of all that diversity; each faith tradition was singing the same song in a deliciously different voice: God is love.

Eventually, the inner conflict between skepticism and devotion melted. I became reconciled to the paradox: I could acknowledge the tragic misuses of religious authority in history and current affairs, while falling to my knees in awe of the stunning beauty at the heart of the mystical poetry in each tradition and the redeeming power of its teachings on peace and justice.

I left home in my teens and moved to the Lama Foundation, an intentional spiritual community in the mountains of Northern New Mexico, where Ram Dass created *Be Here Now*, the groundbreaking book that translated three thousand years of Eastern thought into a contemporary American vernacular and turned an entire generation on to a journey of awakening.

At Lama I was exposed to the world's primary spiritual traditions and several lesser-known ones. I chanted the name of God in Arabic with passionate Sufis, in Sanskrit with ecstatic Hindus, in Hebrew with Kabbalists, and in Latin with Christian mystics. I participated in Native American sweat lodges and silent Buddhist meditation retreats. I met yogis and swamis, lamas and roshis, sheikhs and murshidas, progressive rabbis and radical priests. I took initiation in at least four different lineages that have traditionally wished to eradicate each other from the face of the earth. At Lama, all faiths were welcomed as equally valid means for building a relationship with the Divine. Lama ruined everything for me. How could I commit to a single way after having seen the holy beauty shining from the heart of every one of God's houses?

Since that time, my task has felt clear: to help build bridges between the world's faiths. As a spiritual writer and translator of the Spanish Christian mystics, a religious studies professor, and a practitioner of many spiritual traditions, I have spent my life responding to the call to honor diversity and celebrate unity among all paths that lead us home to love.

I can identify with almost every religious orientation on the planet (including agnosticism). I have embraced my Jewish heritage more fully as I grow older, observing the weekly Shabbat (Sabbath) and carving out sacred time each fall to celebrate the High Holy Days with my community. I have been connected with Sufism since I first encountered the teachings of Murshid Samuel Lewis and Hazrat Inayat Khan as a teenager and experienced the ecstasy of dances of Universal Peace and *zikr*. The philosophy of Buddhism makes more sense to me than any other path, and I have been practicing mindfulness meditation for over thirty years. I believe that Jesus Christ was more than just a very wise rabbi and a nice guy: I feel in my heart that he was a true vessel for the Divine and continues to hold that light in this world, so I guess that makes me a kind of Christian. I have been devoted to the Indian saint, Neem Karoli Baba, whose lineage was Hindu, from the moment I first saw his picture in 1972, and I feel that he has guided my steps throughout my life; he is the one who first exposed me—a Jewish-Sufi-Buddhist—to Christ and Mother Mary, the primary subjects of all the books I have written and translated!

America is the Land of the Consumer. Not only do we help ourselves to the largest portion of the earth's resources while the rest of the world struggles to scrape together the next meal, but we are a culture of dilettantes: We dabble in this religious tradition and that one, chanting om at the end of yoga class, ordering the latest book on how to cultivate prosperity through positive thinking, signing up for a weekend workshop on tantric sex or shamanic journeying. We are conditioned to treat the spiritual life as another commodity, rather than as a discipline of inner transformation with a corresponding commitment to alleviating suffering in the world. Yet, authentic engagement with the perennial wisdom that lies at the heart of the well means we must leap from the lip of the vessel and dive into the unknown.

The late Brother Wayne Teasdale coined the term "interspiritual" to describe "the shared mystic heart beating in the center of the world's deepest spiritual traditions" (*The Mystic Heart*, 2001). This perspective encompasses a much broader scope of shared religious experience than does its predecessor "interfaith" movement, which focuses more on the dialog between the established institutionalized religions than on an intermingling of their common heart. Genuine interspiritual dialog demands that we draw deeply on our inner knowing and show up for the hard work of understanding. It requires that we not only study and discuss religions other than our own, but that we commit to a disciplined practice in more than one tradition, immersing ourselves in the well of wisdom they offer, allowing these encounters to change us from within.

The sacred scriptures of all faiths call us to love as we have never loved before. This requires effort, vigilance, and radical humility. Violence is easier than nonviolence, yet hate only perpetuates hate. The wisdom teachings remind us that love—active, engaged, fearless love—is the only way to save ourselves and each other from the firestorm of war that rages around us. There is a renewed urgency to this task now. We are asked not only to tolerate the other, but also to actively engage the love that transmutes the lead of ignorance and hatred into the gold of authentic connection. This is the "narrow gate" Christ speaks of in the Gospels. Don't come this way unless you're willing to stretch, bend, and transform for the sake of love.

God of Love pays homage to the mystical and social justice teachings at the common core of the world's three great monotheistic religions: Judaism, Christianity, and Islam. Rather than skimming the cream off the surface of each faith and homogenizing them beyond recognition, we are looking for those teachings and practices that unify, rather than divide us. In a world fractured by an ever-renewed demonization of "the other," and fueled by age-old misunderstandings between the Children of Abraham, it is my hope that this book will serve as a reminder of their mutual dedication to lovingkindness as the highest expression of faith. The eleven chapters explore the issues I see as most essential to this quest.

Each chapter is divided into four parts. The first part serves as a kind of "invocation," in which I invite the reader into a personal relationship with the subject. You may or may not identify yourself as the second person I refer to, but my goal is to be as inclusive as possible, so that even people who do not consider themselves to be religious in any way can find a relevant point of access to these wisdom streams.

The second section is an overview of the subject from the perspective of the three Abrahamic faiths, in which I identify their respective positions and attempt to find the common ground between them. It is important for the reader to know that I have not made an effort to be comprehensive in my selection of material. I may have excluded biblical teachings and Quranic references that you would see as essential. I am looking at these issues through my own lens, by definition colored by my own experiences, biases, and wishful thinking.

The third section is memoir. This is the riskiest part for me. All my previous books have been translations of or reflections on the wisdom teachings of others, and I have avoided sharing episodes from my own life or exposing my personal beliefs. Yet what I crave when I read about the spiritual path is stories about real people who, like me, have wrestled with the Divine in the effort to break through to the ultimate. And so this time I offer glimpses from my own journey, not as someone who has arrived somewhere, but as a fellow traveler immersed in the ongoing adventure. I also include stories of people I know and love, who represent a particular aspect of the question at hand.

In the last section, I have selected exemplars I feel embody the primary qualities of the spiritual value the chapter illumines. I have chosen biblical characters and historical figures, rather than contemporary beings, because living people are still works in progress. These narratives are hagiographic, rather than strictly factual. The word "hagiography" refers to accounts of the lives of saints and other holy women and men who are considered to have been specially imbued with the sacred. As such, they are often elevated and set apart from the rest of us, and their function as guides on our own path backfires because we cannot relate to them. So I have tried to make these luminaries as accessible as possible while upholding what was most holy, impeccable, and revolutionary about their lives.

If I have been overly reverential in these pages, let me assure you that it is not only an attitude I take with established holy people; I see almost everyone I know as extraordinary in some way. My husband calls it "Mirabai's Master Syndrome." I am always introducing people as "a brilliant poet," "a gifted painter," "the finest meditation teacher I have ever met," "the mother of that amazing child I told you about," "the most influential animal rights activist west of the Mississippi." Something in me recognizes something in the other as important and beautiful, and I mention this attribute so that they know that at least one person perceives and acknowledges the light in them. If I were to meet you, I would bow at your feet too.

> *You shall love the Lord your God with all your heart and with all your soul and with all your might.*
>
> Deuteronomy 6:5

Love is patient, love is kind. It does not envy, it does not boast, it is not proud. It is not rude, it is not self-seeking, it is not easily angered, it keeps no record of wrongs. Love does not delight in evil but rejoices with the truth. It always protects, always trusts, always hopes, always perseveres. Love never fails. But where there are prophecies, they will cease; where there are tongues, they will be stilled; where there is knowledge, it will pass away.

1 Corinthians 13:4–8

God is love, from love the world became,
And back to love does everything return;
Love binds the different atoms into forms,
Love holds the cells of bodies as a unity,
Makes possible the marvels of growing life,
Turns man into a miniature universe,
And congregates all people in brotherhood;
From love, the complete panorama of life –
Its absence leads to death, to war, to fratricide.
This is no mystery to the awakened heart;
Peace on earth to men of universal will,
Who rise above their selfish limitations
And see the world as God would have them see.

Murshid Samuel Lewis, *The Jerusalem Trilogy:*
Song of the Prophets

TOWARD THE ONE
The Unity of the Divine

*Hear, O Israel: YHVH is our God, YHVH is the One and
Only. You shall love YHVH your God with all your heart,
with all your soul, and with all your resources.*

Deuteronomy 6:4–5

*And Jesus said, The first of all the commandments is, Hear, O
Israel: the Lord our God is one Lord: And thou shalt love the
Lord thy God with all thy heart, and with all thy soul, and
with all thy mind, and with all thy strength: this is the first
commandment.*

Mark 12:29–30

*Say: He is Allah,
The One and Only;
"Allah, the Eternal, Absolute."*

Qur'an 112:1–2

My house shall be called a house of prayer for all people.

Isaiah 56:7

The Nameless Has a Thousand Names

YOU HAVE THE urge (yet are unable) to catch hold of the One and tether it to the altar, where you have been taught to believe the One belongs. You cannot name the One (though you try, calling it God or Goddess, Allah or Cristo, Mother or Lord). You discover that the One cannot rightfully be referred to as He (though tradition requires that you assign a symbolic gender to the formless). You are incapable of wrapping up the Holy One and presenting it to yourself like a toy or a sandwich, a list of rules or a reward.

You may have been conditioned to claim the One for your people alone, but then you see Him everywhere (everywhere!): in a corner of the airport where a man unrolls a small rug and bends to press his forehead, nose, both his hands and all his toes to the ground in submission; in the storefront church of the inner city where poor people sing and weep at the same time; in the grandmother lighting the Sabbath candles and welcoming the Bride of Israel. You recognize your God as everyone's God.

And not only among Jews and Christians and Muslims do you see the reflected face of the One. When the climber reaches the summit and gazes out at a thousand miles of mountains and valleys, there is the One. When the mother pushes through shattering pain to give birth, and the infant sucks in his first breath and expels his wild wail, there is the One. When the father drops to his knees in the military cemetery after burying his son and wraps his arms around his own heaving chest, there is the One. In our first kiss, in our final embrace, there is the One.

The One shows up in Native lodges and Hindu temples, in the deep quiet of Zen meditation halls and in the ecstatic whirling of dervishes. The One whispers through the words of the poets, through the curving lines of painters, sculptors, and woodcarvers; through symphony and hip-hop, Gregorian chant, hymns in praise of Mother Mary, devotional songs to Lord Shiva; through tobacco and cornmeal offered at dawn to the Great Spirit. The One makes an appearance in the heart of the self-described atheist, who gasps in wonder at the beauty of an unexpected snow that fell during the night, carpeting the garden with jewels of frozen light.

The One reveals itself as the compassionate Father and the protective Mother, as unrequited Lover and loyal Friend, residing always at the core of our own hearts, and utterly invisible. The One transcends all form, all description, all theory, categorically refusing to be defined or confined by our human impulse to unlock the Mystery. And the One resides at the center of all that is, ever-present and totally available.

You remember, and forget, and remember again: beckoned with a thousand names, limited by none, the God you love is One.

One God

> *You shall know this day and take to your heart that YHVH,*
> *He is the God—in heaven above and on the earth below—*
> *there is none other.*
>
> Deuteronomy 4:39

FROM THE HEART of Judaism, Christianity, and Islam springs the primordial affirmation of the oneness of the Divine, proclaiming the existence of a Supreme Being who created all that is and continues to take an interest in the whole of creation. This belief in one God is monotheism. Judaism, Christianity, and Islam are the world's primary monotheistic faiths, and they each trace their spiritual lineage to a common ancestor: the biblical patriarch, Abraham.

Abraham was born into a tribal culture that related to the sacred in the form of innumerable individual entities requiring flattery and placation to gain good fortune and resolve problems. But Abraham carried a yearning for connection with the heart of the universe, for a living relationship with Ultimate Reality. He took a radical stand in asserting the existence of one unutterably holy, all-loving God, a being whose omniscience, omnipotence, and omnipresence are equal to His unconditional compassion and perfect justice. This God alone, Abraham claimed, is worthy of worship.

The Holy One made a personal appearance to Abraham in the desert, offering a simple covenant in which the Children of Abraham were invited to take refuge for all time: "I will be Your God and you will be My people." In spite of the many ways in which Jews, Christians, and Muslims have disagreed about the form this covenant should take over the course of millennia, the three religions share a core faith in the absolute singularity of the Divine.

Within each faith tradition, a vast array of beliefs is represented. Some Orthodox Jews insist that every word of the Torah was handed directly to Moses from the mouth of the Holy One on Mount Sinai, and that all 613 commandments are to be obeyed to the letter. There are Jews who do not believe in the existence of a personified God and identify themselves as Jewish simply by virtue of their cultural heritage, a heritage in which they take pride. For some Christians, Jesus Christ is the Son of God and inseparable from the Divine Substance. For others, Jesus Christ was a righteous and loving human being, who modeled the most important teachings on how to be a just and benevolent person in this world. Many Muslims pray five times a day and uphold all the other pillars of faith prescribed in the Qur'an, but others choose to maintain a private relationship with Allah in the temple of their own hearts.

The holiest of all Jewish prayers is the *Shema*, recited by observant Jews each morning and evening, and affirmed by others in key moments of their lives: *Sh'ma Yis'ra'eil Adonai Elocheinu Adonai Echad*. The traditional rendering of this sacred phrase is "Hear, O Israel, the Lord your God, the Lord is One." Yet there are important nuances missing from this version.

The true name of God is too holy to pronounce, and so is frequently represented in the Hebrew Bible by the four letters YHVH, which stand for *Yod He Vov He*. This is how the Holy One first described itself to Moses from the midst of the Burning Bush. YHVH is generally translated as "I am that I am," yet Hebrew scholars agree that the verb "to be" in this context refers to past, present, and future. In other words, "I am that which is, was, and shall be." The Holy One is a dynamic, ever-present reality, rather than a remote Deity. And it requires an active relationship. We are invited not only to "listen" but to engage.

The word "Israel" means "wrestling with God." An alternative translation of the *Shema* from the Jewish Renewal Movement may more accurately represent the radical monotheism Judaism proclaims: "Listen, O you who struggle with the Infinite: All is One." We grapple with the absolute unity of being, while dedicating ourselves to its manifestation in the duality of everyday life.

The *Shahada* in Islam mirrors the *Shema* in Judaism. This is the primary declaration of faith for Muslims, repeated many times a day: *La ilaha illallah*: "There is no God but God." Sufism (the mystical expression of Islam) offers a more encompassing definition: "There is *nothing* but God." From this vantage point, reality is a unified field of Being; nothing is separate from Allah.

The Gospel of Thomas is one of the noncanonical texts of the New Testament, discovered in the Egyptian cave of Nag Hammadi in 1945. It consists of sayings of Jesus, from the perspective of God. Perhaps too mystical for the institutional Church of the third century, this Gospel was not included by the Council of Trent when they finalized the Christian canon. In Logion 77 of Thomas's gospel, Jesus says:

> *I am the Light that is above them all.*
> *I am the All; the All Came forth from Me*
> *and the All attained to Me.*
> *Cleave a piece of wood, I am there;*
> *lift up the stone and you will find me there.*

Called by many names—and by no name at all—the God of Judaism, Christianity, and Islam is One God. It is the Ground of Being, the Absolute, beyond all form yet dwelling within the multiplicity of creation, inscrutable and supremely alive.

Getting to Know the Unknowable

> *Whichever way you turn there is the face of Allah.*
> *Allah is omnipresent and all-knowing.*
>
> Qur'an 2:115

WHEN I WAS a teenager, I yearned to know the Unknowable and spent most of my energy trying to cultivate a connection to God. I memorized the *Fatiha* (the opening lines of the Qur'an), participated in *zikr* (Sufi chanting) and Dances of Universal Peace, read Rumi and Ibn 'Arabi, and studied Arabic calligraphy. I learned Hasidic chants and familiarized myself with the Kabbalistic Tree of Life, lit the candles of Shabbat and invoked the *Shekhinah* (the indwelling feminine Presence of God). Like Salinger's fictional Franny, I attempted to keep the Jesus prayer going in a never-ending mental loop: "Lord Jesus Christ, have mercy on me." It wasn't that I feared Hell; I was wagering that if I could just keep his name on my mind, the Prince of Peace would enter my heart.

Not only that: I practiced hatha yoga and engaged in such vigorous breathing exercises that my face went numb. I learned to play the harmonium and accompanied myself in hours of chanting Hindu divine names: Krishna, Lord of Love; Kali and Durga, manifestations of the Divine Mother; and Hanuman, embodiment of devotion. I sat in silence on my black *zafu* practicing *zazen*, read the sutras of the Buddha and the aphorisms of Lao Tzu. I fingered the 108 sandalwood beads of my *mala* under my desk at school. I knelt at my bedroom altar, contemplating the statues of the deities and the framed faces of the gurus, and I called out to the Holy One with every fiber of my being.

This intensity might have had something to do with the fact that my big brother, Matty, had died of cancer when he was ten and I was seven, blowing open the first doorway to the Mystery, and that my first love, Phillip, had been killed in a gun accident when we were thirteen, pushing me into the Mystery's arms. Also, my parents had recombined partners and my family was in flux.

All of which had coalesced in a tendency toward altered states and spiritual longing.

One day when I was sixteen, as I was carrying groceries from the car to the house, I had an epiphany: the God I was worshipping in as many forms as I could get my hands on was actually a formless Absolute, beyond the beyond the beyond. Even ascribing ultimate qualities to the Divine—such as omnipotence, omniscience, and omnipresence—fell short of the fathomless mystery I had glimpsed. Any attempt to define this sacred reality violated its very nature. I had painted myself into a metaphysical corner. Any way I turned, I left the imprint of my own mental limitations. My only hope was to banish all thoughts of God the instant they arose, now and forevermore. I resolved to tear down the pictures of all the saints and masters plastered on my bedroom wall, get rid of my sandalwood carvings of Krishna and my jade Buddhas, and pack up all my spiritual books, just as soon as I finished putting away the food.

This terrifying confrontation with Unnameable Truth was quickly and mercifully followed by an insight: the same Supreme Reality that surpassed all understanding was accessible through every Sanskrit chant, Hebrew prayer and Christian hymn, through Buddhist meditation retreats and affirmations of the merciful and compassionate nature of Allah, through deep silence and unbridled song. By way of the many, I had encountered the One—over and over again–and

I hadn't even noticed. It was subtle, and it required the engagement of subtle sensibilities.

In that moment, a held breath inside me let go. I still hoped that one day I would merge into the Oneness, but for now I was content to remain apart, in the illusion of separation, where I could adore what mystical theologian Rudolf Otto called the "Wholly Other." From that day on, I no longer saw any conflict between form and formlessness. All the sacred images and spiritual concepts were nothing more than approximations of the boundless source of love, and nothing less than roadmaps home to that love. How could I deny any of them? How could I ever again fall for the notion that any one of His reflections was the only one?

Smashing Idols

IN BOTH THE Jewish and the Muslim traditions there is a story about Abraham that does not appear in the Scriptures, yet illumines the Patriarch's unique task in communicating the essential unity of the Divine. In Judaism, such teaching stories are known as *midrashim*.

It is said that Moses received two Holy Books on Mount Sinai: one written, and one oral. The Oral Torah is a work in progress: each of us contributes to the body of sacred wisdom teachings whenever we engage with the inner meanings that emerge from deep Torah study, and one of the fruits of this process is *midrash*. Historically, Islam embraced many of the teachings of the rabbis that illumined certain sacred truths also proclaimed in the Qur'an, and incorporated them into Islamic tradition. There is no more fundamental spiritual orientation in either Judaism or Islam than the Oneness of God.

In this legend, it is roughly 2500 B.C.E. in Ur, Mesopotamia, which is now Northern Iraq. Abraham is a young man whose father, Terah, is an idol maker, known throughout the region for his stone effigies. People come from afar to purchase these carvings and make offerings to them. Disturbed by the emphasis on commerce and the apparent lack of spiritual connection, Abraham devises a scheme.

One day an old woman delivers a basket of bread to Terah's workshop and offers it at the feet of the idols, entreating them to bless her family in return. When darkness comes, Abraham sneaks into the workshop with a hammer and smashes all but the largest of the idols. He places the hammer in the hand of the remaining effigy, and quietly closes the door behind him. In the morning, when Terah discovers the damage, he roars with rage.

"Who has done this?" he demands of his son.

"Father," Abraham says, "you're not going to believe what happened! A woman brought a basket of bread, and the gods began to fight over it. The biggest one here prevailed over them all, and claimed the entire offering for himself. I've never seen anything like it. An epic battle, really."

Terah stares at his son as if he were insane. "That's impossible," he sputters. "These idols have no power. They are made of stone."

"*Then why worship them?*" Abraham asks.

The young man is condemned as a heretic. His punishment: to be burned to death. But Abraham sits calmly amid the flames, chanting the name of the One God all through the night, and when the door to the village furnace is opened the following morning, he emerges unscathed.

It might be tempting to view this as a story about the ignorance of polytheism and the superiority of monotheism. This would be a mistake. Not only does such an interpretation reinforce a legacy of bullying of indigenous spiritual cultures by dominant religious institutions, it misses the spiritual point. Abraham's smashing of the idols represents the courage to destroy the false idols we worship in place of the Divine: money and success, addictive substances and addictive relationships, the image of our own holy selves as victim or failure. The miracle of Abraham remaining unharmed inside the fire represents the blessings that come rushing in to support us when we dare speak truth to power.

ALL CREATION PRAISES GOD
Stewardship of the Earth

The currents rush,

The mighty rivers roar,

And the ocean's breakers

Thunder and proclaim:

"Yah! Is most powerful!

Your creation is witness

To the sacred and eternal

Beauty of Your house.

Psalm 93

Look at the birds of the air; they do not sow or reap or store

away in barns, and yet your heavenly Father feeds them. Are

you not much more valuable than they? Can any one of you

by worrying add a single hour to your life? And why do you

worry about clothes? See how the flowers of the field grow.

They do not labor or spin. Yet I tell you that not even Solomon

in all his splendor was dressed like one of these.

Matthew 6:26–29

*He created the human being. He taught him the clear
explanation. The sun and the moon are to keep count. And
the stars and the trees both prostrate. And the heavens he has
exalted. And he has set in place the Balance: that you be not
defiant in the Balance. Set up the weighing with justice and
with equity and skimp not in the balance. And he has set the
earth in place for the human race. On and in it are many kinds
of sweet fruit and date palms with the sheaths of a fruit tree
and grains, possessors of husks and fragrant herbs. So which
of the benefits of the Lord of you both will you deny?*

Sublime Qur'an 55:1–12

The Temple of the Wild

YOU HIKE UP an alpine trail that opens into an aspen grove
and drop to your knees in a pool of sunlight. You close
your eyes and begin to apologize to the Holy One:

God, you whisper, *I do not hear your voice in church. The
hymns sound like the tunes they play on game shows while the
contestants are trying to think up the answers.*

You open your eyes and stroke the tassels on a tuft
of blooming buffalo grass. *I do not see your face, Lord, in
the lamentations and exaltations of the Psalms, or in the stri-
dent exhortations of the prophets, or in the bloody history of the
Children of Israel.*

You tilt your face upward, peering through the dap-
pled shadows of the aspen leaves. *Neither prostrating myself five times a day nor continuously repeating Your Name*

seems to connect me to You, Allah. I have failed to tether myself to a single one of the pillars of faith You have provided.

You press your palms against the moist undergrowth.

But here in the wild places, Holy One, I bear witness to the earth as she bears witness to Your glory with every breath she takes. Here I find You everywhere: in the intertwining arc of two hawks dancing their love dance overhead; in the spores of a mushroom that explode into the air when I tap on its spotted cap; in the aroma of decomposing berries beneath a juniper tree; in the slanted light of late afternoon sun as it passes through a stand of scrub oak; in the white-tailed deer as she glances up, nose quivering, then returns to her communion with a patch of clover. I gasp in awe at the majesty of Your world, oh my God. It is perfect. You are perfect.

And I, Lord, am imperfect. Or, at least, that is how I feel when I try to settle into the pews of the church, press myself down on the prayer rug in the mosque, trick myself into showing up for services at my parents' synagogue. I feel like a fraud.

Until I get back to the beach and here You are: cresting the whitecaps of each wave with Your love; here in the desert as the sun rises and the slickrock is bathed in Your love; here in the pasture where I have walked out after dinner to feed my horses, who check my pockets for apples with their velvet muzzles, and You look at me, through their eyes, with the eyes of Your love. I hear Your footsteps as I am running through open fields. I smell Your skin when I take shelter under a ponderosa pine during a snow flurry. It is the wind through the canopy of the rainforest that has taught me to pray.

You finish making amends to the Holy One. You stand up, rub the grass stains on the knees of your jeans, and feeling much better, hike on, heading toward the tree line.

You Are My Tenants

The land is mine and you are but aliens and my tenants.
Throughout the country that you hold as a possession, you
must provide for the redemption of the land.

Leviticus 25:23–24

And he called him and said to him, "What is this I hear about
you? Give an account of your stewardship, for you can no
longer be steward.

He who is faithful in a very little thing is faithful also in
much; and he who is unrighteous in a very little thing is
unrighteous in much.

You cannot serve both God and money.

Luke 16:2,10,13

For He it is Who has made you khalifa on earth,
and has raised some of you by degrees above others,
so that He might try you by means
of what He has bestowed on you.
And thereupon We made you their khalifa on earth,
so that We might behold how you act.

Qur'an 6:165

THERE HAS BEEN some disagreement among the Judeo-Christian-Islamic family about the nature of our relationship with nature. In Genesis 1:26 we are told that when He had finished creating the heavens and the earth and all creatures except human beings, the Creator said, "Let us make humans in our image, and let them rule over the fish of the sea and the birds of the air, over the livestock, over all the earth and over all the creatures that move along the ground."

This passage has been exploited by all three monotheistic religions as an excuse for devastating the environment. We have not understood that dominion implies responsibility and stewardship. Rather than view our power over the rest of creation as a sacred trust, to be handled with reverence, we have muscled our way through the universe, bullying our fellow creatures, poisoning the atmosphere, and ravaging the earth.

If we believe that the Holy One handed us the world like a cosmic crackerjack box, then we may feel entitled to stuff the entire contents into our mouths and grab the prize at the bottom. If, on the other hand, we embrace creation as our family, we may feel compelled to do everything in our power to wrap it in a cloak of protection and feed it with our own hands. Like loving parents, we will put the needs of our dependents above our own needs, and their joy becomes our joy.

The great first-century rabbi Yochanan ben Zakkai taught that "if you have a sapling in your hand, and someone says to you that the Messiah has come, stay and complete the planting, and then go to greet the Messiah" (Avot d'Rebbe Natan 31b). A hadith of the Prophet

Muhammad says, "When doomsday comes, if someone has a palm shoot in his hand he should plant it."

We are called to balance the cultivation of our own spiritual liberation with our dedication to tending the earth that sustains us.

At the heart of Judaism, Christianity, and Islam is a sense of radical awe in the face of creation, accompanied by the impulse to glorify the Creator. According to both the Bible and the Qur'an, all created things are designed to praise God in their own special way. The prophet Isaiah proclaims: "The mountains and hills will burst into song before you, and all the trees of the field will clap their hands" (Isaiah 55:12–13). The twentieth-century sage Abraham Joshua Heschel says that Judaism exudes "a kind of drunken joy and surprise at the beauty and incomprehensible sublimity of the world, of which man can obtain but a faint intimation." It is that same sense of exaltation, Heschel goes on to say, that also "seems to manifest itself in the song of the birds."

We are urged to back up this childlike wonder with a mature sheltering response. Our challenge is not only to recognize the face of the Creator in the beauty of creation, but also to serve the Divine by taking care of the land, the air, and all beings that dwell with us here. In the tradition of mystical Judaism, this is part of *tikkun olam*, the sacred charge to join our energy with the energy of the Holy One in an effort to restore the broken cosmos to wholeness.

Muslims strive to erase the lines between the sacred and the secular, and make each moment a living prayer. Allah transcends all that He created, and yet is "closer to Him than (his) jugular vein" (Qur'an 16). Each sunrise, each meal, every challenge and triumph in work and human relationships, are opportunities to praise God. The meaning of the word "Islam" is "surrender": the *surrender* of our entire being to the Holy One. Again and again, we bow down in loving submission before such a glorious God, and all creation bows with us. Which of the blessings of the Lord, the Qur'an challenges us, will you deny?

Walking

> There is One Holy Book, the sacred manuscript of nature,
> the only scripture which can enlighten the reader. . . . All
> scriptures before nature's manuscript are as little pools of
> water before the ocean.
>
> Hazrat Inayat Khan, "There Is One Holy Book"

I HAVE ALWAYS felt most fully at home with myself while walking in the woods and deserts, beaches and meadows, city parks and village streets. Most days, no matter what the weather is, I rise up against the tyranny of tasks and disengage from whatever project or problem is screaming for my attention. In the silence this revolutionary act creates, I open the door, call my dog, and head up into the Sangre de Cristo Mountains to remember who I am.

The Bible proclaims that we are created in the image of God, which says to me that we, in our authentic core, resemble God. When I walk, especially in nature, I become more fully who I am: that is, a divine being. So the flow goes like this: reconnecting with the earth reconnects me with myself; remembering who I am, I remember the Holy One. And, in paying attention to the rest of creation, I recognize my interconnectedness with the web of all created beings. I am fed from the breast of the earth, grateful for the unconditional generosity of the Mother/Father of us all.

My friend Elaine is a priestess of the Temple of Hiking. For Elaine, getting lost is the highest sacrament. Not one to take herself too seriously even in the most solemn circumstances, Elaine meets each unanticipated adventure with good cheer. She celebrates the opportunity to meet the Holy One in the wild places of the earth and does not presume to be in charge of these sacred encounters.

Elaine describes the moment in which it dawns on her that it has been an hour or more since she had any sense of where she has come from or where she is headed, and that she may not find any semblance of an established trail any time soon. The sun might be going down, first stars popping into the dome of the sky, and the temperature dropping by tens of degrees in as many minutes. Elaine's response is to sit down with her back against a ponderosa pine and eat an apple.

More often than not, Elaine deliberately steps off the trail and bushwhacks her way up the mountain, or back down again. This practice, she says, keeps her fully in the present moment. "It's too easy to go unconscious when I walk on familiar paths," Elaine explains. "There is a freedom in making my own way through the wilderness, forging my own connection with what is." In this way, Elaine embodies the surrender of Islam: she submits to the Divine, which she encounters everywhere in nature, and this relationship leads her home.

My husband Jeff is a surfer. He grew up on the beaches of Southern California, and the ocean has always been his second mother. When he is in the water, he feels held by the Sacred Feminine. The very first time he paddled out, waited for a wave, stood up, and rode the surf back to shore, he felt he had encountered the Divine. This experience has repeated itself a thousand times since. For Jeff, surfing is spiritual practice. A man of few words, Jeff describes it like this: "I sit; I wait; I breathe. I stare into the void. And then, when a wave comes, it's a gift."

In 1968, when he was nineteen, Jeff was drafted into the army and shipped off to Vietnam. It was surfing, he claims, that saved him. The night before he left Jeff had a dream. Even though he had been assigned to serve as a helicopter mechanic, in the dream he saw himself surfing, and he woke with a clear sense that this would be how he would spend his tour of duty. When his sister wept as she hugged him goodbye, Jeff told her about the dream and assured her that he would be safe.

After a few months tinkering with helicopter engines, flying around with the pilots to test his repairs, and spending nights patrolling the bunker line as a perimeter guard, Jeff was sent to the company physician to treat bone spurs on his feet, which prevented him from wearing standard issue combat boots. Instead, he wore tennis shoes with his uniform. Jeff enjoyed this sanctioned opportunity for rebellion, but it made his superiors bristle.

As the doctor examined Jeff's feet, she asked him how his condition had developed. "They're surfer knots," he explained. "We all get them."

"You're a surfer?" she said. "Why didn't you say so? I'll have you transferred to the coast, and you can serve as a lifeguard."

And so, Jeff spent the remainder of his tour on the beaches of Chu Lai, tending traumatized soldiers who were sent to the beach to recuperate from the horrors of the front. In between saving men who went out swimming too drunk to make their way back to shore and sitting quietly with men who shook so hard they could not speak, Jeff rode the waves of the South China Sea, safe in the arms of the Mother.

Brother Francis and Sister Hildegard

HILDEGARD OF BINGEN (1098–1179) was a revolutionary abbess who saw God flaming forth from the earth and the sky, from broken-open seedpods, and from the heart of stones. She celebrated "the greening power of God" as *viriditas*, the animating life force within all creation, filling the world with verdant, juicy, extravagant holiness.

Born into the lush Rhineland river valley, Hildegard was surrounded by fecundity all her life. It was easy for Hildegard to recognize the Holy Spirit as the agent of the

Divine, moving the breath of God through all of creation, causing everything to germinate and sprout and burst into bloom.

Hildegard was an herbalist, a healer, a social critic, a composer, and a visionary artist whose illuminations illustrate the complex architecture of the cosmos, and the special place humanity holds at the center of all that is. "God loans all of creation to humankind for our use: the high, the low, everything," Hildegard warns. "If we misuse this privilege, God's Justice gives creation permission to offer humankind a reminder."

Although celebrated in her lifetime for the wisdom of her visions and the beauty of her music, Hildegard of Bingen may have been too wild to be officially sanctioned by the Church, and was never canonized. But nine centuries after her death, people of all faiths still look to this German nun as a model for praising God as the Mother, who "kneaded the elements together" to create this magnificent world, "sustaining it with wetness" and "bearing its weight with her own strength."

Almost a hundred years after Hildegard lived, a wealthy young nobleman named Francesco stripped the fine garments from his body and walked naked into the arms of the unknown. He traded wealth and privilege for the hand-spun robes of a monk, gathered a circle of like-minded brothers and sisters, and embraced a life of voluntary simplicity. Saint Francis became a beacon for humanity in our quest to discern what is healthy and holy in our relationship with the rest of creation. He made poverty look like ecstasy. He approached caring for the poor and the sick as an adventure. He showed us that every single creature is our sibling and that interspecies communication is our birthright.

Francis of Assisi initiated a radical reform of the Church, restoring Christ's own commitment to the values of sustainable living, compassionate action on behalf of the most vulnerable among us, and a joyful embrace of our place in the web of all life. This twelfth-century Italian friar is revered as the patron saint of ecology and the epitome of holy childlike joy. What few of us realize is that Francis suffered for the choices he made. He was condemned by his family and ostracized by society. His order of brothers grew so large in Francis's own lifetime that it succumbed to the perils of institutionalization and betrayed his founding vision. Francis often felt isolated and misunderstood. The more precarious his mission became, the more tightly he held onto it, and the more his disappointment grew.

Even the saintly Saint Francis endured doubt and gave in to self-righteousness. Even a genius like Hildegard was silenced by the authorities. And so, when we begin to lose hope in the face of the magnitude of environmental catastrophe we are facing, we may rightfully offer ourselves and each other an extra dose of encouragement. Of course, we bleed for the bleeding earth! We would do anything in our power to alleviate her suffering, yet are overwhelmed by the complexity of the issues. We are more than willing to lessen our impact on the environment, yet feel helplessly plugged into the machinery that is driving her to the brink of destruction. This can be a recipe for despair, but it doesn't have to be.

In Genesis it says that when God finished bringing every aspect of creation into being, "He saw that it was good." The wisdom of the Abrahamic traditions would suggest that we embrace the bounty of this good earth, and yet never take more than our share of her harvest. By practicing mindfulness about what we consume, we avoid becoming mindless consumers. Small gestures of voluntary simplicity become prayers of devotion as we endeavor each day to walk lightly on the land, cultivate harmonious relationships with our fellow creatures, defend the purity of our water and our air, and glorify the Great Spirit by revering its presence in all of creation.

RELUCTANT PROPHETS
The Divine Summons

The One Who Is says:
Can two walk together without meeting? Does a lion roar in
the forest if it has no prey? Does a beast let out a cry from its
den if it has not trapped its meal? Does a bird suddenly fall
to the ground unless snared? Does a trap spring up from the
ground without having caught something? When a shofar
sounds in a town, do the people not worry? Can misfortune
befall a place if the One Who Is has not caused it?
Indeed, the One Who Is does nothing without first revealing it
to the divine servants, the prophets.

Amos 3:3–7

I baptize you with water for repentance, but one who is more
powerful than I is coming after me; I am not worthy to carry
his sandals. He will baptize you with the Holy Spirit and
with fire.

Matthew 3:11

*Do they say: "He is only a poet"...? Do they say, "He has
invented it himself"? Indeed, they have no faith. Let them
produce a scripture like it, if what they say is true!
Were they created out of the void? Or were they their own
creators? Did they create the heavens and the earth? Surely
they have no faith! Do they hold the treasures of your Lord,
or have control over them? Have they a ladder by means
of which they overhear him? Let their eavesdropper bring
positive proof!*

Qur'an 52:30–40

Mouthpiece of the Divine

THE CALL DOES not come softly. It bangs the shutters of
your heart and wakes you from a deep sleep. It drenches
your conscience; your cup overflows with the fire of global
suffering. You have no choice but to respond, to rise from
your bed and rush to the town square and sound the bell
reserved for emergencies: "Wake up!" you cry out. "The
world is burning!"

You would do anything to avoid this task. You are
busy, tired, overwhelmed with problems of your own.
Besides, you are shy. You dread making a spectacle of
yourself. You are not qualified to address the social injustices and environmental catastrophes you see looming
everywhere. You are no scientist. You have not studied
economics or practiced community development. You
will sound ignorant, hysterical, and no one will listen.
Pick someone else.

But the call is unrelenting. A tangible presence beats like wings against your heart. A voice whispers in your ear: *Why are children starving when there is enough for everyone? Get the human family to divide things up more equitably. They are worshipping the false idols of money and power. They turn the Great Mystery into a commodity and call it God. People are good; they just don't realize that their individual actions matter. If they knew, they would change. Tell them. Do it now.*

You roll over in bed, try to adjust your pillow more comfortably, count backward from one hundred, and pray for sleep. Then come images of bombs exploding, dismembered body parts, the vacant stares of unanticipated death, kitchen utensils poking out from a pile of rubble where only an hour ago a pot of barley stew simmered on a stove.

A legion of crises rushes onto the stage of your mind, clamoring for attention: human beings sold like goats into forced labor or sexual slavery; girls forbidden to receive an education; AIDS, malaria, and dysentery ravaging entire communities too poor to defend themselves; villages where even a cupful of clean water is a luxury only dreamed of; hurricanes, earthquakes, and tidal waves transfiguring vast landscapes and unraveling personal histories.

Where do you begin to respond to the needs of the human family, the urges of the Holy Spirit, the unrelenting demands of the God of Love? Once you have realized, with every fiber of your being, that everything is interconnected and there is only one of us, how do you turn away from the face of suffering in any of its many guises? The death of a single child is the death of your child. One educated woman lifts the whole world out of ignorance. A communicable disease stopped in its tracks saves us all.

So you do what you have always done when you are confused, helpless, sorrowing. You sit up and close your eyes and become quiet. You stop chattering and begin to listen. Then you let your listening soften into being, and you bear witness to your breath as it flows in and out, like the surf. From this space of stillness, tender compassion for the human predicament washes over you. You feel protective of the well-being of the earth herself. One or two issues rise to the surface of your troubled mind: gang violence, maybe, or the shrinking of the polar ice caps, sanctioned torture, or immigration reform. When you are finished with your meditation, you will pick one. You will stand up; you will speak out—you will not be afraid— and then you will get to work.

The voice of the Holy Spirit is whispering now: "Don't worry," she says, "I will be with you."

Then the Spirit of the Lord will rush upon you, and you will prophesy with them and be turned into another man.

1 Samuel 10:6

Jesus said to them, "Only in his hometown, among his relatives and in his own house is a prophet without honor."

Mark 6:4

Recite in the name of your Lord who created—created man
from clots of blood. Recite! Your Lord is the Most Bountiful
One, who by the pen taught man what he did not know.

Qur'an 96:2–5

Hineni

NOT ALL PROPHETS do as they are told. Not at first, anyway. When the call comes, most of them turn left and then
right: "Who, me?" they murmur. If the call is a true one,
the voice of the Holy Spirit will roar: "Yes, you!"

Even then, the prophet will haggle with the Holy One.
"There must to be someone better suited to speak for the
Divine." But the God of Love is a patient God. The God
of Love calls once, twice, three times. Only then does the
prophet square her shoulders, gird her loins, open her
hands, and say, "*Hineni.* Here I am."

The history of Judaism, Christianity, and Islam
abounds with accounts of great beings who trembled when
they were confronted with the presence of the Divine and
given a task of global dimensions. Traditionally, this reluctance is implied, rather than stated, yet when we read
the scriptures with an open heart, we can feel the anguish
behind the submission.

Exodus 3 describes the encounter between Moses
and God in the burning bush. Moses, a Jewish orphan
raised as an Egyptian in the palace of the pharaoh, rises
up in opposition to injustices against the Israelite slaves.
When the pharaoh hears of his foster son's revolutionary

behavior, he threatens to have Moses executed. Forced to flee the only home he has ever known, Moses takes refuge in the mountains of Midian, where he marries the daughter of a local holy man and embraces the simple life of a shepherd. He would gladly remain anonymous forever, but one day the Holy One beckons him from the heart of a desert bush that bursts into flames before his eyes.

"Moses," He calls. And He repeats, more loudly this time: "Moses!"

"*Hineni*. Here I am," says the shepherd.

The voice identifies itself as the God of Abraham, Isaac, and Jacob, and reveals the prophet's task: Moses is to return to Egypt and rescue his suffering people from the yoke of slavery and deliver them to a land flowing with milk and honey.

All Moses needs to do, says the Lord, is to explain to the pharaoh that the God of the Hebrews "happened upon us," and then request that the Children of Israel be allowed to go into the wilderness for a few days to praise the God of their ancestors. Following his audience with the supreme ruler of Egypt, Moses is to instruct the Israelites to gather a few belongings and follow him into the unknown, because the voice of God issued from a bush that burned but was not consumed and told them to do this.

"But they will not believe me," protests the reluctant prophet, "and they will not heed my voice. They will say, 'Hashem (the Holy Name) did not appear to you.'"

God shows Moses a series of miraculous signs by which he will be able to convince the people that he is leading them in the name of the Divine. Still, Moses resists. For one thing, he suffers from a speech impediment, and cannot think of a less likely candidate to serve as the mouthpiece of the Lord. He tries to explain this to the Holy One, but God dismisses his objections.

"Who makes a mouth for man," Hashem points out. "Who makes one dumb or deaf, or sighted or blind? Is it not I? So now go!" He commands. "I shall be with your mouth, and teach you what you should say."

And so Moses goes, and God goes with him, just as He promised.

Jonah was worse. In this biblical parable, the Holy One chooses Jonah to enter the city of Nineveh, where the people have fallen into corruption and violence, and let them know that God is not pleased with their behavior. But, says the Lord of Love, if they repent, He will in His infinite compassion forgive them. Jonah, the quintessential reluctant prophet, does not think the people of Nineveh are worth saving, and so he tries to sneak away in the hope that the Holy One will not notice.

The Holy One notices. Jonah sets sail on a ship bound in the opposite direction from the place where God sent him. A sudden storm blows up and threatens to drown everyone on board. The crew casts lots to see who should be sacrificed to God to appease His anger. Jonah pulls the short stick and is tossed into the sea. Instead of drowning, the prophet is swallowed by a giant fish, where he languishes in its belly for three days and nights before being ejected onto the shore.

In the darkness of the fish's bowel, Jonah comes face to face with his own emptiness. Suspended between life and death, any sense that he has control falls away. Jonah has no choice but to surrender to the unknown. Stripped of who he thought he was, he is able, at last, to be filled with God. In the end he gets out of his own way so that he may spread the word of the God of Love.

It is said that the Divine does not choose the wealthy and powerful to be prophets. He picks farmers and illiterate caravan drivers, orphans and poor Jewish virgins. He favors the ones who stand up to Him, talk back to Him, the ones who challenge the divine directive. When the angel of the Lord told the matriarch Sarah that she was going to become the mother of many nations, Sarah laughed. She was long past the age of childbearing, and the Patriarch Abraham was even older. When her son was born the following year, they named him Isaac, which means "laughter."

Although twelfth-century Greman visionary Hildegard of Bingen began having visions at an early age, she saw that when she shared this with her family they were afraid, and so she learned to hide her gifts. As Hildegard grew older, the divine voice became increasingly urgent, accompanied by a fiery light. The more she resisted, the more Hildegard was consumed by the inner fire. Eventually, she grew so ill she could not get out of bed.

"Speak and write!" the voice commanded. At last, Hildegard reached for a quill and a scroll, and the prophetic messages came pouring through. For the rest of her life, Hildegard was a conduit for what she called "the Living Light," producing a trove of music, art, healing remedies, and cosmological schema.

Mary of Nazareth did not aspire to be the Messiah's mother. When the angel Gabriel appeared to inform her that she was highly favored and was going to give birth to the Son of God, Mary was skeptical. She pointed out that she was a virgin, engaged to be married to a carpenter. The angel explained that the Holy Spirit would come to her and that Mary would be overshadowed by the Most High, and from this encounter she would be quickened with the child Jesus.

"Nothing is impossible with God," the angel proclaimed. Mary surrendered. "Here I am," she said, "the handmaid of the Lord." Mary's assignment did not end with Christ's conception. Once she had made the divine agreement, Mary remained steadfast, nurturing her holy son through his ministry of love, until he drew his final breath and she held his tortured body in her arms one last time.

In the Gospel of Luke, a seer named Simeon meets the Holy Family on the steps of the Temple in Jerusalem where they have come to have the baby Jesus circumcised, a holy rite of the Jewish tradition. Simeon predicts the fate of the Christ Child, and then he turns to Mary, saying "And a sword will pierce your own heart, too."

"The prophets of Israel," Karen Armstrong writes in *A History of God*, "experienced their God as a physical pain that wrenched their every limb and filled them with pain and elation." Adrienne von Speyr says that the prophets are "inconsolable." It is easy to see why they might have been reluctant to answer the call.

It is not only the biblical prophets who paid this price for responding to the divine summons. Prominent modern activists, imbued with the teachings of the God of Love, risked their lives on behalf of the most vulnerable among us: Mohandas Gandhi; Dr. Martin Luther King; Edith Stein; Etty Hillesum; Bishop Oscar Romero, and an increasing number of moderate Muslims, such as Tawakkol Karman of Yemen, who won the Nobel Peace Prize in 2011.

Countless women and men—known and unknown—stand up every day to give voice to the voiceless—not because it seems like the right thing to do, but because they have no choice: The call comes storming through the gates of their hearts like an invading army, and they stand aside. In the act of surrendering to the Divine, the prophet relinquishes comfort, control, and any hope of being understood.

Hollowed Out

EVERY ARTIST I know admits to being possessed from time to time, taken over by a presence that is vaster, wiser, and more creative than they are. Some call it the Muse. Some see it as the collective unconscious. But some, if pressed, would admit that there are times when they feel that they are being used as conduits for the Divine. The creative act carries a prophetic quality.

I confess: This is how I sometimes feel when I write. I become hollow and a higher being settles in and gets to work. I do not know the things she knows. I cannot write my own thoughts as swiftly as she expresses hers. I am not as loving or as clear as she is. She has a better sense of humor, and she doesn't care what other people think. In those moments—or afterward, really, because while it is happening I am not reflecting on the process—I feel as though I was being used for a greater purpose. How else could I account for the bewildering fact that, as a Jew with ecstatic Sufi inclinations, a lifelong devotion to a Hindu guru, and a committed Buddhist meditation practice, I have published almost a dozen books on Christian mysticism? Father Bill, my iconographer priest friend, says that this is exactly why God chose me: I love Christ, yet I stand outside the tradition and have none of the baggage that comes with membership. Unencumbered, I can lightly step out of the way.

It happens sometimes when I'm teaching, too. I walk into a room where I am scheduled to speak, and it feels as though I park myself back on the threshold. By the time

I take my place at the front of the room, I am empty, and that better voice shows up and speaks through me. I am captive and I am captivated. I can't wait to hear what she's going to say next, but I cannot hold onto it. Afterward, I hardly remember a thing she said. I feel spent, but satisfied. Used, and used up. Each time I am struck with the sense that this is what I'm here for.

In Christianity, this sacred presence is seen as the Holy Spirit, and its essence is sometimes personified as Wisdom. In Judaism it is acknowledged as *Shekhinah*, who traveled alongside the Israelites as they made their way through forty years in the wilderness, appearing as a pillar of cloud by day and a pillar of fire at night. For most of us, this inflowing of sacred knowingness feels like grace: we did nothing to deserve it, and we bow in gratitude at its feet.

This may sound more supernatural and rarified than it is but I believe we are all prophets, each one a mouthpiece for the Divine. This is no more extraordinary, and no less miraculous, than the fact that we can communicate through language, give birth, or compose music. Whenever we say yes to the inrush of spirit, when we stand against injustice no matter how uncomfortable it makes us, when we allow the sacred mystery a place of honor at the table, we are showing up for the prophetic experience. This is not magic, and it is not reserved for some kind of mystical elite: It is our birthright as human beings. It is our highest calling and our most urgent task.

Seal of the Prophets

THE PROPHET MUHAMMAD was a natural contemplative. Born in Mecca in 570 CE of the Quraysh tribe,
Muhammad became an orphan at the age of six. A poor
but loving uncle adopted him, and Muhammad began
working when he was still a child. In his midtwenties,
Muhammad fell in love with the wealthy widow who
owned the caravan he managed. Although Khadija
was fifteen years older than Muhammad, she asked
him to marry her, and they were very happy together.
Muhammad became a successful merchant, yet his heart
was never fully engaged in commerce. He was much
more interested in the God of Love.

Sixth-century Arabia was a harsh environment. The
nomadic tribes of the desert culture paid homage to a host
of invisible spirits in the hope of appeasing the tempera-
mental *jinn* and easing the brutal conditions of their own
lives. An underlying climate of mutual suspicion nursed
tribal loyalties and often erupted in blood feuds. Material
goods were scarce, bandits were on the rampage, and
gambling was out of control. Sexual promiscuity was epi-
demic among men, while women were treated as chattels.

Islamic teachings hold that it was Adam who first
built the holy *Ka'bah*, in praise of his Creator. Tradition
claims that later, when Sarah banished Ishmael and his
mother, Hagar, Abraham accompanied them to Mecca,
where he rebuilt the sacred shrine and rededicated it in
the name of the One God. By the time Muhammad appeared on the scene, however, any concept of a single

all-knowing and all-loving Supreme Being had been forgotten, and Mecca was a pilgrimage center dedicated to
the worship of minor deities, depicted in stone effigies.
Religion had become big business.

In between trading expeditions, Muhammad would
retreat to the caves outside Mecca to fast and pray. One
night, when the Prophet was forty, he was meditating on
Mount Hira when an angelic presence filled the cave with
radiance. It revealed itself as the angel Gabriel, messenger
of the One, who had also appeared to the Old Testament
prophet Daniel to give him "skill and understanding"
regarding his visions, and to the Holy Mary in the New
Testament to announce that she was to give birth to the
Prince of Peace.

The disembodied voice commanded the contemplative to "Recite!" Although Muhammad was innately curious and had learned a great deal from the Jews, Christians,
and other tribal peoples he encountered along his caravan
routes, he had never learned to read or write. Trembling,
Muhammad tried to explain to the angel, "I am not one
who recites."

The angel enfolded the man in a powerful embrace.
"Recite!" he repeated. Again Muhammad protested: "I
am not one who recites." The angel squeezed him again,
even harder this time. For the third time the angel in-
sisted, "Recite!"

Gasping, Muhammad finally gave in. "What shall
I recite?"

At that moment, the opening lines of the Holy Qur'an began to come flooding through, in a series of divine revelations that lasted twenty-three years. Muhammad's initial experience of revelation is known in Islam as "the Night of Power." It is so holy that Ramadan, the cherished yearly practice of fasting, commemorates this sacred event.

At first, though, Muhammad wondered if he might be going crazy. Had he really been visited by an emissary of the Divine, or was he possessed by a *jinn*, masquerading as an angel? Shaken and bewildered, he fled the cave and stumbled home in the moonlight. Pausing to catch his breath and calm himself, Muhammad looked up and saw the angel's face filling the space between earth and sky.

"Muhammad," Gabriel spoke, "You are the messenger of Allah."

Like all the prophets before him, Muhammad could not imagine himself worthy of such a mission. This humility seems to be one of the marks of an authentic prophetic soul. But reluctance is only a starting place, and must not be the final word. The path of each prophet begins with a moment of surrender, followed by a radical receptivity to the divine voice.

After his vision of Gabriel in the night sky, the Prophet rushed home to his wife and laid his head in her lap. "Cover me!" he cried. Khadija wrapped her shawl around her husband and held him until he stopped shaking.

"Rejoice, dear husband," Khadija soothed him, "and be of good cheer. You will be the prophet of this people."

At this moment, Khadija, who had always revered her husband's natural kindness, modesty, and insight, became the first convert to Islam. She never doubted Muhammad's mental stability or questioned the authenticity of his experience in the cave of Hira. Reassured by his wife's loving certainty, Muhammad began to let go of his fear and open himself to an attentive listening for the divine voice.

Muslims do not worship Muhammad. He is a prophet, rather than an incarnation, of God. Because of his pure submission to God alone, Muhammad serves as the model of the perfect human being. His holiness lies not in his own being, but in his pointing away from himself and toward the Holy One.

The root of the word "Islam" is *salam*: peace. The literal translation of "Islam" is "surrender," yet a more expansive version is "the peace that comes with utter surrender to God." The Qur'an teaches that Islam is not the latest iteration in a series of monotheistic faiths, starting with Judaism and followed by Christianity. Rather, it is the primordial religion, an affirmation of what humans have always known, and yet continuously forget: There is only one absolute reality. Muslims believe that God tried to teach us the truth of monotheism through Moses, and when the people once again fell into unconsciousness He sent us Jesus to wake us up. When we lost our way yet again, He sent one last messenger, Muhammad, known in Islam as "the seal of the Prophets," to offer a final reminder of the One God.

La illaha il Allah, Muslims pray: "There is no God but God." *Muhammad rasullallah*: "And Muhammad is His messenger." The Sufi practice of internally repeating the name of God is known as *dhikr*, "remembrance." Its outer expression, which generally takes the form of communal chanting, is called *zikr*. We are made to praise the One. We remember, and forget, but we always remember again. This is the gift of the prophets: to remind us of what is real.

LONGING FOR THE BELOVED
The Illusion of Separation

At night on my bed I longed
for my only love.
I sought him, but did not find him.
I must rise and go about the city,
the narrow streets and squares, till I find my only love.
I sought him everywhere
but I could not find him.

Song of Songs 3:1–2

O Lord, you Supreme Trickster! What subtle artfulness you
use to do your work in this slave of yours. You hide yourself
from me and afflict me with your love. You deliver such a
delicious death that my soul would never dream of trying to
avoid it.

Teresa of Avila, *The Book of My Life*

I've had enough of sleepless nights,
Of my unspoken grief, of my tired wisdom.

Come my treasure, my breath of life,
Come and dress my wounds and be my cure.
  Mevlana Jalaluddin Rumi, "I've Had Enough"

The Fire of Separation

THERE IS A longing that burns at the root of spiritual practice. This is the fire that fuels your journey. The romantic suffering you pretend to have grown out of, that remains coiled like a serpent beneath the veneer of maturity. You have studied the sacred texts. You know that separation from your divine source is an illusion. You subscribe to the philosophy that there is nowhere to go and nothing to attain, because you are already there and you already possess it.

But what about this yearning? What about the way a poem by Rilke or Rumi breaks open your heart and triggers a sorrow that could consume you if you gave in to it? You're pretty sure this is not a matter of mere psychology. It has little to do with unresolved issues of childhood abandonment, or codependent tendencies to falsely place the source of your wholeness outside yourself. The longing is your recognition of the deepest truth that God is love and that this is all you want. Every lesser desire melts when it comes near that flame.

You realize that not everyone experiences this. For some people, the spiritual journey is not so dramatic. It's less about the overwhelming desire for union with some invisible Beloved than it is about quietly waking up. It's about developing compassion, rather than suffering passion. There are people who never doubt that God is with them, and so there is nothing to long for.

But there are those, like you, who have felt the Divine move like an ocean inside them, and, incapable of sustaining an unbroken relationship with that vastness, feel they have been banished to the desert when the wave recedes. There is a tribe of holy lovers, who have tasted the glorious sweetness that lies on the other side of yearning, when the boundaries of the separate self momentarily melt into the One, before the cold wind of ordinary consciousness blows through again, and restores your individuality. You would risk everything to rekindle that annihilating fire. You would leave your shoes at the door and run after the cosmic flute player, if only you could hear that music one more time.

You give up everything for one glimpse of the Beloved's face. You sneak into his chamber in the middle of the night and say, "Here I am. Ravish me." But when you awake the next morning, swooning and alone, you realize you missed the entire encounter. You throw your clay cup on the cobblestones and it shatters. You thought you would marry, bear babies, make a career in broadcasting. You wander city streets during siesta hour and wonder where he is sleeping. Your longing and your satisfaction are reciprocal. The moan of separation is the cry of union.

The Paradox of Union

> *The spiritual marriage . . . is like rain falling from the sky into*
> *a river or pool. There is nothing but water. It's impossible to*
> *divide the sky-water from the land-water. When a little stream*
> *enters the sea, who could separate its waters back out again?*
> *Think of a bright light pouring into a room from two large*
> *windows: it enters from different places but becomes one light.*
>
> Teresa of Avila, *The Interior Castle*

MYSTICS THROUGHOUT THE ages and across cultures have borrowed the language of romantic love to express the way they simultaneously desire and connect with the sacred. "The longing is the Christ," said the great Sufi poet Kabir. The heart that reaches out for the Divine is filled in the very act of offering its emptiness. Solomon's Song of Songs is both a lament and a celebration of this love-longing. It never mentions the name of God. Such naming would be a reduction of the vast mystery. Blasphemy. The Divine is the Beloved. The bridegroom who ignites the soul with His love and then disappears, leaving her blazing and crazy with longing.

This is holy madness. It is anguish and it is bliss. It tears down the walls of the heart and dissolves the trappings of propriety. It turns the soul into Mary Magdalene, the beautiful outcast, who storms the halls of powerful men, demanding to see the One who turned her whole world into blinding light. When she finds him seated at the table, she prostrates herself before Him and, with great tenderness, washes His feet with her tears, dries them with her hair, kisses them, and anoints them with precious oil.

One of the great paradoxes of the mystical path goes like this: The soul spends all her life longing for union with the Divine. And when at last she reaches the object of her desire, she disappears into Him. There is no one left to enjoy the reward. No distinction between lover and Beloved. There is only love. The lover of God craves annihilation; she wants to become nothing. The lover of God desires only to lose himself in love, leaving no trace of a separate self. This longing is illogical and out of control. It is all-consuming and it is all we really want. It is absurd, and it is our birthright.

"Wash yourself of yourself," says Rumi. "Be melting snow." In Kabbalah, this process is known as *bitul hayesh*, "nullification of one's somethingness," and is consciously cultivated through prayer. In the Christian tradition, the union of the soul with God in love is called "bridal mysticism." And in Sufism, it is *fana*, where the soul attains complete unity with Allah. In every case, there is a dying of the false self into the truth of the Divine.

"God, whose love and joy are present everywhere," said Angelus Silesius, the seventeenth-century German mystic and poet, "cannot come to visit you unless you are not there."

John of the Cross is the sixteenth-century Christian mystic who coined the term "Dark Night of the Soul." For John, the spiritual life is a matter of extricating ourselves from our attachment to feeling and thinking about God in habitual ways so that we can meet God as He truly is. John describes this encounter as a secret rendezvous of the soul with her Beloved that unfolds in the deepest part of the night. Dazzled by divine radiance, our ordinary faculties of sense and reason are engulfed and dismantled. This, John points out, is a cause for celebration.

When John of the Cross lay dying, a priest came to administer last rites. John, a devout Catholic and a priest himself, waved away the ritual. "Please," he said, "read to me from the Song of Songs." This scripture, which dispenses with religious phraseology and uses the language of love, best reflected the saint's own sense of his imminent reunion with the One for whom he had been longing all his life.

The great Sufi teacher Hazrat Inayat Khan placed special emphasis on the sacred phrase *Ishq Allah Ma'bud Allah*, which he translated as "God is Love, Lover, and Beloved." In *Love, Human and Divine*, Inayat Khan writes, "The Sufis say that the reason of the whole creation is that the perfect Being wished to know Himself, and did so by awakening the love of His nature and creating out of it His object of love, which is beauty."

The story of Layla and Majnun is a seventh-century love legend that comes from the northern Arabian Peninsula. In this tale, a Bedouin poet named Qays falls in love with a woman of his own tribe, called Layla. When Qays asks for her hand, her father refuses on the grounds that the marriage would be a scandal, and he marries her off to another man. Qays loses his mind with longing for his beloved and retreats to the desert where he writes love poems in the sand with a stick. The villagers name him *Majnun*, the "madman." Layla dies of a broken heart.

Like the Song of Songs, the story of Layla and Majnun is an allegory for the relationship between the soul and the Divine. It maps the trajectory from the intoxication of finding the Beloved to the anguish of losing the Beloved, and the inevitable ego-death that must occur before the two can be reunited in the boundless field of love. It illumines the path of holy madness, the path trod by fools of God.

This love dance is not some rarified state reserved for long-dead saints and the occasional living master. We do not have to go insane with longing. Few of us will relinquish the last traces of ego and walk away from our life in the world. We can feed the fire of divine love by cultivating simple practices that expand our hearts and raise our consciousness, such as meditation and chanting, reciting ancient prayers or conversing with the Beloved, in silence or in lifting our voices, in solitude or in community. "There are a hundred ways to kneel and kiss the ground," says Rumi.

Longing may be our legacy, but wholeness is our birthright. It lies at the heart of the disappointments and delights of everyday life. In weeding the garden and burning the toast. In falling asleep alone or enfolded in the arms of another. In reading poetry instead of watching the news. In missing the grandmother you adored and becoming the father you never had. In weeping for the suffering of the oppressed, the degradation of the planet. In singing, in drumming, in rejoicing against all odds.

This Beautiful Wound

> *Sometimes an arrow of love pierces the heart and penetrates the deepest core of the soul so that she doesn't know what has happened or what she wants, except that all she wants is God. She feels like the arrow has been dipped in a poisonous herb that makes her reject herself for love of him. She would gladly give up her life for him. It's impossible to explain the way God wounds the soul or to exaggerate the agony it causes. It makes the soul forget herself entirely. Yet this pain carries such exquisite pleasure that no other pleasure in life can compare to that happiness. The soul longs to die of this beautiful wound!*
>
> Teresa of Avila, *The Book of My Life*

DEATH HAS BEEN my own gateway to the numinous. I did not pick this path. I have simply experienced an unusual number of tragic losses, which propelled me to plunge into spiritual practice as if my life depended on it, which in many ways it did. As the years went by, death after death continued to reveal traces of grace. As long as I can remember, my sorrow has been the catalyst for my longing for God.

Yet the inner harvest these multiple losses yielded did not prepare me for the avalanche that would sweep through my life, annihilating everything in its path. The year I turned forty, the day my first book came out, a translation of *Dark Night of the Soul* by the sixteenth-century

Spanish saint John of the Cross, my fourteen-year-old daughter, Jenny, was killed in a car crash.

Suddenly, the sacred fire I had been chasing all my life engulfed me. I was plunged into the abyss, instantaneously dropped into the vast stillness and pulsing silence at which all my favorite mystics hint. So shattered I could not see my own hand in front of my face, I was suspended in the invisible arms of a Love I had only dreamed of. Immolated, I found myself resting in fire. Drowning, I surrendered, and discovered I could breathe under water.

So this was the state of profound suchness I had been searching for during all those years of contemplative practice. This was the holy longing the saints had been talking about in poems that had broken my heart again and again. This was the sacred emptiness that put that small smile on the faces of the great sages. And I hated it. I didn't want vastness of being. I wanted my baby back.

But I discovered that there was nowhere to hide when radical sorrow unraveled the fabric of my life. I could rage against the terrible unknown—and I did, for I am human and have this vulnerable body, passionate heart, and complicated mind—or I could turn toward the cup, bow to the Cupbearer, and say, "Yes."

I didn't do it right away, nor was I able to sustain it when I did manage a breath of surrender. But gradually I learned to soften into the pain and yield to my suffering. In the process, compassion for all suffering beings began unexpectedly to swell in my heart. I became acutely aware of my connectedness to mothers everywhere who had lost children, who were, at this very moment, hearing the impossible news that their child had died. I felt especially connected to mothers in war zones, although I lived in safety and abundance in America.

Interdependence with all beings has never again been an abstract concept to me. I am viscerally aware of my debt to every blade of grass. Innumerable, unexpected blessings emerged from the ashes of my loss: a childlike wonderment and gratitude in the face of the simplest things: a bowl of buttered noodles, reading poetry to my husband in bed, two horses prancing across the field behind our house. These are the blossoms that unfold from my growing relationship with the Mystery of Love. This is the holy potion that has been given as the antidote to my brokenness.

Grief strips us. According to the mystics, this is good news. Because it is only when we are naked that we can have union with the Beloved. We can cultivate spiritual disciplines designed to dismantle our identity so that we have hope of merging with the Divine. Or someone we love very much may die, and we find ourselves catapulted into the emptiness we had been striving for. Even as we cry out in the anguish of loss, the boundless love of the Holy One comes pouring into the shattered container of our hearts. This replenishing of our emptiness is a mystery, it is grace, and it is built into the human condition.

Few among us would ever opt for the narrow gate of grief, even if it were guaranteed to lead us to God. But if our most profound losses—the death of a loved one, the ending of a marriage or a career, catastrophic disease or alienation from community—bring us to our knees before that threshold, we might as well enter. The Beloved might be waiting in the next room.

The Immovable Spot

THE GREAT SIXTEENTH-CENTURY Spanish mystic Teresa of Avila was not always in love with God. In fact, during her first twenty years in the convent, she alternately envied and disdained the girls who openly wept with the pain of separation from their Beloved. Teresa prided herself on being a practical person. "God dwells among the pots and pans," she declared. If one of the young nuns in her care displayed a tendency toward altered states of consciousness, Mother Teresa would yank her from the chapel, stick a broom in her hand, and order her to sweep the portico until the delusion passed.

One day, however, during her thirty-ninth year, the Holy One rushed the boundary Teresa had built around her heart. The efficient nun was bustling through the halls of the convent, readying the place for an upcoming festival, when she noticed a statue of Christ at the pillar unceremoniously propped against a wall. Irritated, Teresa bent to pick it up. Suddenly, her eye caught his, and she was transfixed.

Christ's face radiated unbearable suffering and unconditional love. Even as his back was bent and scored with lacerations, the blood dripping into his eyes from the thorns that pierced his scalp, he gazed at Teresa with a tenderness that felt absolutely personal and offered her his undivided attention. Never had she felt so fully seen. Never had she imagined herself worthy of such a love as he was pouring upon her.

Teresa's knees buckled and she slid to the floor at his carved feet. Then she kept going. She unfolded her body in full prostration, pressing her face to the ground, arms stretched above her. Her heart overflowed and she began to cry. She cried tears of longing and tears of fulfillment. She wept with remorse for never having loved Christ as he deserved to be loved, and she wept with supplication that he never, ever leave her.

Like the Buddha as he sat in meditation under the Bodhi Tree, vowing not to move from that spot until he had broken through to enlightenment, Teresa drove a bargain with her Lord. She told him that she would not get up until he gave her what she wanted: the strength to adore him and never to forsake him again. Once the dam had broken, all the tears of a lifetime cascaded through her heart, and Teresa lay weeping for a long time. When she was spent, she rose transfigured. From that moment on, Teresa of Avila began to undergo the stream of visions, voices, and raptures for which she is so famous.

Near the end of her life, Teresa finally experienced the union of love she had so fervently longed for—in what she referred to as "the seventh chamber of the interior castle," where the Beloved dwells at the center of the soul. Once this love had been consummated, all the supernatural phenomena fell away, the ecstatic states and levitations ceased, and Teresa became a fully integrated being. Like the bodhisattva in the Buddhist tradition, Teresa found the highest expression of spiritual love in dedicating herself to the service of others.

RADICAL WONDERMENT
Faith in the Absence of Proof

*I saw the Lord sitting upon a throne, high and lifted up; and
the train of his robe filled the temple.*

*Above him stood the seraphim. Each had six wings: with two
he covered his face, and with two he covered his feet, and with
two he flew.*

*And one called to another and said: "Holy, holy, holy is the
Lord of hosts; the whole earth is full of his glory!"*

Isaiah 6: 1–3

*And amazement seized them all, and they glorified God and
were filled with awe, saying, "We have seen extraordinary
things today."*

Luke 5:26

*Remember your Lord in yourself
Humbly and with awe.*

Sublime Qur'an 7:205

At the Feet of the Mystery

WHERE ONCE YOU were fed on the Word, now you find the Holy One in the center of a luminous silence. In the face of that radiance, all concepts vanish. You rest in the emptiness of unknowing. The hymns and prayers that used to fill your heart with the presence of God have become dried husks. *Where did the juice go?* you muse, more curious than distressed. The doctrines that had sustained you are beginning to sound ridiculous. Even as you recite the familiar liturgy, you find yourself perplexed: *What in the world does that mean?* you ask.

You dare not speak these questions aloud. Not to your parents. Not to your priest or minister, not to your sheikh or your rabbi. It took these people decades to establish a solid foundation of belief amid the ever-shifting tectonic plates of this life. To them, this dropping down into emptiness is not good news. It looks like a crisis of faith. They will rush in to fix you. But you are intrigued by your own unraveling. You would like to see what comes next. It is a relief to know nothing, to want nothing. *If this is an ailment,* you think, *may I never recover.*

It is as if one day you leaned on the edifice of recycled spiritual sensations and established theological constructs and the whole thing came tumbling down. As if the curtain had gone up, the house lights switched on, and the audience vanished. There you are, in an empty theater, with the light in your eyes and a sweet silence in the air. You dangle your legs over the stage like a child, and blink in wonderment. *Oh,* you say. *I got so lost in the play I forgot what was real.* It's not as if the drama was that great to begin with. It was a tragedy: everyone died in the end.

Melting

> *Do you have faith in him that he will return your grain and gather it to your threshing floor?*
>
> Job 39:12

> *But if God so clothes the grass of the field, which today is alive and tomorrow is thrown into the oven, will he not much more clothe you, O you of little faith?*
>
> Matthew 6:30

> *If you put your whole trust in Allah, as you ought, He most certainly will satisfy your needs, as He satisfies those of the birds. They come out hungry in the morning, but return full to their nests.*
>
> Tirmidhi

JUDAISM EXTOLS THE unknowability of the Divine. The Holy One is so holy that nothing true can be said of Him. Jews are encouraged to question God, to winnow God language and shake out the essence. This legacy of doubt as a valid spiritual practice originates with the biblical story of Jacob wrestling with the angel.

On a journey of filial reconciliation, Jacob sends his family across a river and spends the night alone on the other side. As he lies down to rest, an angelic being appears out of the darkness and picks a fight with him.

The two wrestle all night, and the supernatural stranger is unable to overcome his human opponent. Jacob's hip is dislocated in the struggle, but he does not give up. As dawn breaks, the angel insists that Jacob release him. Recognizing his divine nature, Jacob refuses to let him go without obtaining his blessing.

The angel responds by asking Jacob's name. Then he says, "Your name shall no longer be called Jacob, but Israel, for you have striven with God . . . and have prevailed" (Gen. 32:28). Jacob/Israel apprehends the significance of this encounter with the Absolute: "I have seen God face to face, and yet my life has been delivered." He limps away from the experience transformed. He is triumphant, but he carries the wound to remind him of the challenge to overcome illusion and emerge with truth.

Jews embody this legacy of grappling with God. There is merit in the struggle. By refusing to take religious teachings at face value, by approaching the Torah as a living reality rather than a stagnant text, by exposing the sacred to the laser of deep inquiry, the seeker may cultivate an ever-renewing relationship with the Holy One. It is not always comfortable to divest ourselves of limiting concepts and barren practices. It can be terrifying to find ourselves alone with Mystery. Yet it is necessary to undergo periods of radical unknowing.

Judaism is not the only tradition that refuses to see a crisis of faith as a problem. From the perspective of the Christian mystics, an authentic spiritual meltdown is a cause for celebration. It is only then that we are stripped of our attachment to the way the presence of God is supposed to feel, and begin to rest in spiritual nakedness. Divested of our mental constructs about the existence and nature of this God, we come face to face with Ultimate Reality. In the midst of our crumbling, we may not see it as grace. In fact, it looks as though we are giving up on God or, even worse, that God has abandoned us.

On the contrary: The confrontation with unmitigated nothingness, says John of the Cross, is a sign of spiritual ripening. The Dark Night of the Soul signals that the Holy One sees we have matured and are ready for the real spiritual adventure.

> *Just as Abraham made a great feast when his son Isaac was*
> *weaned, so there is rejoicing in heaven when God removes the*
> *baby clothes from the soul. He is setting her down from his*
> *arms and making her walk on her own two feet. He removes*
> *her lips from the milky breast and replaces the soft, sweet*
> *mush of infants with the crusty bread of the robust.*
>
> John of the Cross, *Dark Night of the Soul*

LIKE BABIES BEING weaned, we do not feel ready to let go of our dependency on spiritual goodies and have a direct encounter with the Holy One. We protest. We throw a spiritual tantrum. We strain to regain the high we used to get from prayer and chanting, from ritual and liturgy, but the juice has run dry. We struggle to think our way through the problem of not knowing, but it is, by definition, unsolvable. There is nowhere to turn, no one in whom to confide. We cannot make sense of this darkness to ourselves, let alone communicate the depth and breadth of the anguish to anyone else.

The Dark Night of the Soul is often an intensely private experience, invisible to the casual observer. It may have nothing to do with external circumstances, such as a painful separation, an ominous diagnosis, or the death of a loved one. Yet life-changing losses can be a catalyst for the internal breakdown of our most cherished beliefs. If we tighten against the pain of this process, we may miss the opportunity for personal transformation and spiritual healing that lies in the heart of that fire.

Muslims, too, have a language for this blessed spiritual devastation. "All things in creation suffer 'annihilation' [*fana*] and there remains the face of the Lord in its majesty and bounty" (Qur'an 55:26–27). The corollary of *fana* is *baqa*, a state of continual remembrance of the Divine in each moment—which can only occur when the ego is submerged into the ocean of longing for God.

Faith lies at the heart of the creative tension between forgetting and remembering. In melting into the boundlessness of divine love, we unlearn everything we thought we knew about Allah. Only then, by *becoming* love, do we come to know truly. This kind of faith is not blind, though it strips us of our ordinary apparatus of perception. It is a faith tempered in the fire of experience: the experience of absolute surrender to the Mystery. It cannot be shaken; it is inviolable.

When Rudolph Otto spoke of the numinous, he was pointing to the encounter with divine mystery embodied in Judaism's God-grappling, Christianity's Dark Night of the Soul, and the self-annihilation of *fana* in Islam. For Otto, the numinous experience has two complementary attributes: *mysterium tremendum*, which brings us to our knees in awe of the Wholly Other, and *mysterium fascinans*, an irresistible desire to become one with it. Without presuming to understand the Divine, we nevertheless place ourselves utterly in its hands.

Dazzling Darkness

> *Faith is the bird that feels the light and sings while the dawn is still dark.*
>
> Rabindranath Tagore

> *One morning a beloved said to her lover to test him, "Oh so-and-so, I wonder, do you love me more, or yourself?*
> *Tell the truth, oh man of sorrows!"*
> *He replied, "I have been so annihilated within thee that I am full of thee from head to foot.*
> *Nothing is left of my own existence but the name.*
> *In my existence, oh sweet one, there is naught but thee.*
> *I have been annihilated like vinegar in an ocean of honey."*
>
> Mevlana Jalaluddin Rumi, "One Morning a Beloved Said to Her Lover"

> *But if I am to perceive God so, without a medium, then I must just become him, and he must become me. I say more: God must just become me, and I must just become God, so*

completely one that this "he" and this "I" become and are one
"is," and in that isness, eternally perform one work.

Meister Eckhart

Man's last and highest parting is when, for God's sake,
he takes leave of God.

Meister Eckhart

FOR AS LONG as I can remember I have been in love with
a God I'm not sure I believe in. Part of this reluctance to
claim my faith comes from growing up in a family of secular humanists. It is has been with some chagrin that I
have found my life dedicated to writing, speaking, and
meditating on the object of blame for countless centuries of suffering: God. But this turns out to be a false dilemma. James Farris, priest of the Ecumenical Catholic
Communion, makes this important distinction: "I have
found that those who say they are atheists often reject a
God I could not accept."

The God my parents repudiated is not my God. My
God is too vast to be contained by theology, too mysterious to be defined, too holy to be personified. My God
neither punishes nor rewards, but invites me into a living
relationship that unfolds in the heart of all that is. My God
belongs to everyone, and this belonging connects me to
the web of all life.

My faith is not set in opposition to reason. I have no
trouble reconciling science with spirit. The study of string
theory in particle physics is as holy an endeavor to me as
the practice of contemplative reading of scripture in *lectio*

divina. I am in awe of a Creator who arranged natural selection and endows the bumblebee with the miraculous
ability to defy the laws of aerodynamics and fly. I embrace
the mind as a vehicle for transcending the mind. When it
takes me to the threshold of the Mystery, I have no trouble
jumping off and entering the void.

And yet this God of mine is not mere emptiness. It
is imbued with the energy of love. It is an overflowing
of love into the entire container of the cosmos. I call it
the Sacred, and there is nowhere it is not. I am in awe of
this God of Love, who breaks through ordinary moments
with a dazzling radiance and melts the boundaries of my
individuated consciousness and reminds me that I am not
separate from the source of Love Itself.

While I may be reluctant to assign an identity to this
God I love, I am fully willing to love Him with all my
heart and all my soul and all my mind. I have written this
love on the doorposts of my heart. I arise with its song
on my lips, and I fall asleep with its fingers on my eyelids. I teach this love to my children—which is everyone I
meet—and I drop love letters to my God everywhere I go.

This faith is not predicated on belief. It is informed
by experience—at once ordinary and sublime—and
continuously reinvented through the active process of
unknowing, revitalized by an ongoing encounter with
the Mystery.

Divine Doubters

*For those with faith, no explanation is necessary. For those
without, no explanation is possible.*

Thomas Aquinas

Faith which does not doubt is dead faith.

Miguel de Unamuno

Doubt isn't the opposite of faith; it is an element of faith.

Paul Tillich

*Be patient toward all that is unsolved in your heart. And try
to love the questions themselves.*

Rainer Maria Rilke

THE BINDING OF Isaac, known in the Torah as the *Akedah*,
epitomizes the power of unconditional surrender to the
God of Love. In Genesis, Abraham and Sarah long for the
child divinely promised to them. When, in their extreme
old age, they are blessed with the birth of Isaac, their attachment could not be more profound. The most radical test of faith in all of sacred literature unfolds in this
context.

"Abraham," God calls to the Patriarch one day.
"*Hineni*," Abraham answers, "here I am." God directs
Abraham to take his son to Mount Moriah and offer him
as a sacrifice. The Patriarch ascends the mountain with his
beloved child. "Father?" Isaac calls, as Abraham prepares
the wood and the fire, the knife and the altar. "*Hineni*,"
Abraham replies. Isaac points out that all objects for a ritual slaughter are in place, except for the sacrificial animal.
His father assures him that God will "seek out the lamb

for the sacrifice." Then Abraham proceeds to bind his son and place him on the stone slab.

Even as Abraham stretches out his knife and prepares to plunge it into the heart of the person he loves most in the world, he surrenders to the sacred mystery. That is when an "angel of Hashem" calls to him. "Abraham," he says. "*Hineni*," Abraham replies. The angel commands him to put down his weapon. Then the voice of God informs the Patriarch that because of his unequivocal trust in the Divine—his radical awe of the God of Love—he is released from his terrible task. "And Abraham raised his eyes and saw—behold, a ram!—afterwards, caught in the thicket by its horns; so Abraham went and took the ram and offered it up as an offering instead of his son" (Genesis 22:13). Centuries of religious debate have unfolded in response to this quintessential story of faith in the absence of proof.

It is easy to forget that Isaac was not Abraham's only child. When God does not seem to be following through on His end of the covenant—to make Abraham's descendants as numerous as "all the particles of dust of the earth"—Sarah decides to take matters into her own hands and arrange a sexual liaison between her husband and her Egyptian servant, Hagar. But when Hagar conceives Ishmael, Sarah is overcome with envy and treats Hagar so harshly that the pregnant girl runs off into the desert.

When Hagar collapses beside a spring, weeping, an angel calls out to her, "Where have you come from? Where are you going?" Hagar admits that she is fleeing from her mistress, and the angel informs her that the Holy One has heard her prayer and that she will give birth to a son. Now she must return to Canaan and surrender her will to the divine will. Hagar responds by naming God. "You are the God who sees me," for she said, "I have now seen the One who sees me" (Genesis 16:13). And Hagar calls the place where she saw the One who had seen her, "the Well of the Living One Appearing to Me."

Even Christ grappled with moments of despair. Between his baptism by John on the banks of the River Jordan and the launching of his ministry, Christ retreated to the desert for forty days of fasting and prayer. There he was visited by the spirit of evil, who confronted him with all the reasons he should abandon his divine calling. In the Garden of Gethsemane, the night before his arrest, Christ prayed so hard he sweated blood, while the disciples he had asked to guard him slept instead. "Father," he said, "if you are willing, take this cup from me; yet not my will, but yours be done" (Luke 22:42).

Finally, as he suffered on the cross, Christ cried out to his *Abba*, his Father: "Around the ninth hour, Jesus shouted in a loud voice, saying '*Eli, Eli, lama sabachthani?*' which is, 'My God, my God, why have you forsaken me?'"(Matthew 27:46). Not long afterward, Christ uttered his final words: "And speaking in a loud voice, Jesus said, 'Father, into your hands I commit my spirit.'" Christ's evolution of spirit between abandonment and reunion serves as a model for the universal process of opening the heart, despite every reason not to.

When Muhammad received his first revelation, he thought he must be going mad. But Khadija assured her husband that he was the sanest person she had ever known, and the most humble. It was her faith that kept the Prophet going as his mission of love began to unfold.

As Etty Hillesum, a Dutch Jew, boarded a train from Westerbork in the Netherlands to Auschwitz in Poland, a postcard fluttered from her hand, on which she had written: *We have left the camp singing.* She was gassed to death two months later.

Between her birth in 1914 and her death at the age of twenty-nine, Hillesum had ripened into what Buddhists call a *bodhisattva.* That is, she had unconditionally dedicated her life to alleviating suffering in every being she encountered. In the face of the unspeakable horrors of the Holocaust, she disarmed her heart and poured herself out. "One should want to be a balm on many wounds," she wrote in her diary. And she was.

The diary of Etty Hillesum is a testament to spiritual awakening. The more cruel and terrifying the actions of the Nazi authorities grew, the more serene and centered she became. Like other Jewish contemplatives, such as Edith Stein and Simone Weil, she borrowed the language of Christian mysticism to describe the inner sanctuary she built. "I draw prayer about me like a dark protective wall," she writes, "withdraw inside it as one might a convent cell and then step outside again, calmer and stronger and more collected again."

But hers was not a blind faith. She did not harbor any illusions about the mounting horrors being perpetrated on her people. She was dedicated to facing reality with open eyes and embracing it with open arms. Although she was offered multiple opportunities to escape, Etty was determined to share the fate of her people: certain annihilation.

"By excluding death from our life we cannot live a full life," she writes, "and by admitting death into our life we enlarge and enrich it." Safe in her conviction that the world being brought to its knees by the atrocities of war nevertheless overflows with beauty, Etty resisted the impulse to demonize the Nazis and categorically refused to hate anyone. "My battles are fought on the inside," she admits, "with my own demons."

Etty Hillesum's peace blossomed in proportion to her surrender to what was happening. In the midst of cultivating universal love, she felt God kneeling beside her. "I am so calm it is sometimes as if I were standing on the parapets of the palace of history looking down over far-distant lands. This bit of history we are experiencing right now is something I know I can stand up to. I know what is happening and yet my head is clear." It is this clarity and courage that Etty took with her into the camp and distilled into an elixir to soothe the fears of her people and rekindle their faith, even as they stepped into the gas chambers that would exterminate them.

WELCOMING THE STRANGER
Table Fellowship

*You shall treat the stranger who sojourns with you as the
native among you, and you shall love him as yourself, for you
were strangers in the land of Egypt: I am the Lord your God.*

Leviticus 19:34

*And when was it that we saw you a stranger and welcomed
you, or saw you naked and gave you clothes? Truly I tell you,
just as you did to one of the least of these who are members of
the human family, you did it to me.*

Matthew 25:38

*Serve God . . . and do good to orphans, those in need,
neighbors who are near, neighbors who are strangers, the
companion by your side, the wayfarer that you meet, and
those who have nothing.*

Qur'an 4:36

Welcome Home

LATE AT NIGHT, you think you hear a knocking at the door of your heart. You peer out the window into the darkness, clutch the folds of your robe. Maybe you imagined it. You begin to head back to bed when the knocking comes again, more urgent now.

"Excuse me?" a voice calls. "I'm a little lost. And hungry."

You hesitate for a moment longer, measuring habitual caution against an irrational surge of fearlessness. The scales tip and you throw open your heart-door to greet the stranger there.

"Welcome home," you say.

Only then do you recognize her face. It is God! And she looks exactly like you.

Then there are the nights when you bolt the door of your heart, stuff wads of silicone in your ears and pop a pill so that nothing can reach you. You would like to be available, but your days are long and your cupboards are bare. You aspire to make each act an offering to the Divine, yet sometimes it is all you can do to take out the garbage without bursting into tears. You wish you could see the face of God in everyone always, but your eyes are clouded by longing and disappointment.

Besides, the Holy One has a tendency to hide behind preposterous disguises: he is the homeless man lumbering through the park talking to himself in a loud voice, a pint of Cuervo Gold tucked into the back pocket of his jeans; she is the teenager texting her boyfriend and applying mascara at the stoplight after it has turned green; he is the young father gambling away his children's dinner at the Indian casino on his way home from another day at the sewage treatment plant; she is the elderly woman slowly counting out change at the convenience store when you are late for a job interview, and he is the Very Busy Man who does not give you the job.

You understand that this is why all the sacred teachings remind us to be vigilant: God could pop up anywhere, anytime, and drop His mask. When he does, we must be sure we have treated Him like God, no matter how He was behaving.

The Guest as God

HaShem *appeared to him in the plains of Mamre while he was sitting at the entrance of the tent in the heat of the day. He lifted his eyes and saw: And behold! Three men were standing over him. He perceived, so he ran toward them from the entrance of his tent, and bowed toward the ground. And he said, "My Lord, if I find favor in Your eyes, please pass not away from your servant."*

"Let some water be brought and wash your feet, and recline beneath the tree. I will fetch a morsel of bread that you may sustain yourselves, then go on — inasmuch as you have passed your servant's way." They said, "Do so, just as you have said."

So Abraham hastened to the tent to Sarah and said, "Hurry!
Three se'ahs of meal, fine flour! Knead and make cakes!" Then
Abraham ran to the cattle, took a calf, tender and good, and
gave it to the youth who hurried to prepare it. He took cream
and milk and the calf which he had prepared and placed these
before them; he stood over them beneath the tree while they ate."

Genesis 18:1–8

Jesus said to him, "If you wish to be perfect, go, sell your
possessions, and give the money to the poor, and you will have
treasure in heaven; then come, follow me."

Matthew 19:21

This being human is a guest house.
Every morning a new arrival,
a joy, a depression, a meanness,
some momentary awareness comes
as an unexpected visitor.

. . . .

Meet them at the door laughing,
and welcome them in.
Be grateful for whoever comes,
because each has been sent
as a guide from beyond.

Mevlana Jalaluddin Rumi, "The Guest House"

THE TRADITION OF desert hospitality, cherished by Jews, Christians, and Muslims alike, is an essential portion of the legacy of the Patriarch Abraham. The three travelers who appeared to Abraham in the Torah are, of course, representatives of the Holy One. Some have interpreted them as angels; some identify one in particular as God Himself. Abraham does not quibble; he is the perfect host, and treats every guest as God.

Rashi (the medieval biblical commentator) points out that when *Hashem* shows up in Genesis 18, Abraham is sitting outside his tent, convalescing. Three days earlier, at the age of ninety-nine, Abraham was circumcised, as the Lord had commanded, and this is the point at which "the wound is most painful and the patient most weakened." So it is no small task for the old man to rush around making sure the strangers are given the very best of everything.

Not only that, but when they leave, Abraham escorts the travelers until their destination, Sodom, comes into view. My friend Rick always walks his guests to their car when they leave, opening the doors and waiting until they strap in and drive away before he heads back into the house. When I remarked on how cared for I felt when he did this, he reminded me of the story of Abraham's visit from God, explaining that the Torah teaches us to treat every being as a spark of the Divine.

Each of the three Abrahamic faiths cherishes some version of the Hidden Holy One. In mystical Judaism, it is said that at all times there are thirty-six extraordinary people on the planet, known as *Tzadikim Nistarim*, the Hidden Righteous Ones, whose purpose it is to hold the cosmos together. If even one of them was missing, the world would come to an end. Not only are these righteous beings hidden from the rest of us, but they are unknown even to themselves. Anyone who suspects he might be a *Tzadik Nistar* is definitely not one. They are humble, simple, anonymous people, who serve as exemplars by refusing to claim their specialness.

In the Gospels, Christ conceals his identity on numerous occasions after his crucifixion and resurrection. When Mary Magdalene comes to his empty tomb to anoint his body at first light following the Sabbath, she mistakes her risen Lord for the gardener, and demands to know what the man has done with Jesus. Then he says her name: "Mary." And she falls at his feet, weeping with joy.

Around the same time, two disciples are walking along a road outside Jerusalem, lamenting the catastrophe of their Master's murder, when Jesus sneaks up on them. Lost in grief, they do not recognize him. He pretends to know nothing of recent events, and asks them to tell him about this man they had hoped was the Messiah. The hidden Christ proceeds to interpret all the signs in the Torah that point toward the divine perfection of all that has transpired, and his teachings put their hearts and minds at ease. When they arrive at the village of Emmaus, the disciples invite the traveler to eat with them before continuing on his journey. It is only as he lifts the bread in blessing that they realize who he is. In that moment, Christ vanishes.

Islamic teachings point to the existence of a mysterious being called Khidr, "the Green One," embodiment of the ever-living, always vibrant energy of the spirit. Khidr comes in unexpected forms at unanticipated times, and when he does, he opens a direct channel between the seeker and the sought—the soul and Allah—and initiates us into a dynamic relationship with the Divine. It is said that Khidr instructed Moses and Muhammad, and so is known as the Teacher of the Prophets. Sufis identify Khidr as the Friend the soul longs for, the one whose presence illuminates our hearts with true understanding. We search everywhere for a glimpse of his face, and must remain watchful for signs of his blessings.

The Last Supper of Jesus Christ serves as the very embodiment of Table Fellowship. This dinner, of course, was a Passover Seder. Jesus and the disciples had joined thousands of devout Jews who would come to the Temple in Jerusalem every year to celebrate Pesach, the holy day that commemorates the miraculous escape of the Israelites from slavery in Egypt. It was during this sacred occasion that Christ initiated the tradition of the Eucharist, pouring the Passover wine and breaking the Passover matzo as reminders of his undying love for all who hunger and thirst for the God of Love.

After the meal, Jesus rose from the Seder table, "laid aside his garments" and "girded himself with a towel" (John 13:4). He called for a basin of water and began to wash the disciples' feet. This gesture of tenderness and humility broke open the hearts of his companions, and became a living symbol of one of the highest commandments in Judaism: to love your neighbor as yourself. It was also a reminder to lay aside arrogance and entitlement and be willing to serve any and all beings.

The life of Christ is a mirror for the generous face of the Divine. One Gospel story after the next reveals a God-Man who treated everyone as the embodiment of the Beloved. I have always believed that when Jesus said, "I am the way, the truth, and the light," he did not mean that he was the only one: he meant that we also—each one of us—are the way, the truth, and the light, and that he incarnated to remind us of our essential divinity.

Christ's first miracle was an act of hospitality: he turned water into wine at a wedding where the hosts had run out of libations to serve the guests. On another occasion, when the multitudes gathered to hear him preach in a remote area and grew hungry after many hours of teachings, Jesus urged the disciples to share their meager provisions among thousands of guests. The loaves and the fishes miraculously multiplied (as those with food began to share with those who did not) and fed them all, with food left over.

Christ dines with prostitutes and drinks with tax collectors. He restores sight to the blind on the Sabbath and raises the children of his detractors from the dead. He breaks all the rules to make sure that everyone, everyone, is welcome at the table of the Holy One.

In *A Voluptuous God*, interspiritual author Reverend Robert Thompson quotes from the "Ballad of Judas Iscariot" by poet-mystic Robert Buchanan. After his suicide, the soul of Judas carries his broken body through the spiritual wilderness, in a futile search for a place to lay his burden down. At last, on the point of despair, Judas comes across a house where wedding guests are gathered around a table, eating, drinking, and celebrating. Christ, the Bridegroom of the Holy One, meets his betrayer on the threshold.

> *"The Holy Supper is spread within,*
> *And the many candles shine,*
> *And I have waited long for thee*
> *Before I poured the wine!"*
> *The supper wine is poured at last,*
> *The lights burn bright and fair,*
> *Iscariot washes the Bridegroom's feet,*
> *And dries them with his hair.*

According to Thompson, "the heaven to which Jesus points is the spaciousness within ourselves—one that makes room for those who threaten us, for those who are different, even for those who have betrayed us." In Carlos Castaneda's books, Don Juan speaks of our "petty tyrants," the people who drive us crazy, who offend our most cherished sensibilities, who bring out the worst in us. These people are, of course, our greatest teachers. They belong at the top of our guest list.

In the parable of the Good Samaritan, Christ suggests that the neighbor the Torah commands us to love may not look at all like us. A man is robbed and beaten, and left dying on the side of the road. A priest of his own people crosses the street to avoid him. When a member from another tribe sees the injured man there, he cleanses his wounds with oil and wine from his own flasks, then takes him to a nearby inn and cares for him there. The next day, he leaves enough money with the innkeeper to make sure the stranger's needs are covered until he is well enough to leave on his own. What is Christ's conclusion to this teaching story? "Go and do likewise."

Saint Francis of Assisi is famous for having embraced a leper. Francis suffered from a revulsion to leprosy. But he had an epiphany. A privileged young man, Francis was recently home from the war, grappling with posttraumatic stress disorder. Seeking solace for his inner turmoil, he spent more and more time in solitude and silence.

One day, Francis was riding through the woods when he heard the clattering of a bell, signaling that a leper was in the vicinity, which gave the passerby an opportunity to get out of the way. Before he had time to react, however, Francis had entered the clearing where the leper lay resting. When he gazed down at the man's ravaged face, Francis perceived no difference between the leper and the Lord. He leapt down from his horse and gathered the man into his arms, gently kissing his rotting cheeks and eyelids. Having not only faced his greatest fear but embraced it, Francis was never able to see another being as "other" again. All of creation became his family—even Brother Fire, even Sister Death.

These teachings are not mere allegories: they are instructions. It is not enough to recognize the other as oneself and to grasp our essential interconnectedness with all beings. The real work lies in putting our beliefs into practice.

Not only is everyone welcome at the feast of the Divine; no one anywhere should ever go hungry. True Table Fellowship means making a commitment that everybody in our community has enough to eat. Compassion is not a matter of feeling pity for the poor; it is a direct engagement with the roots of poverty, a willingness to sacrifice our own comfort for the well-being of someone else, an unqualified identification with those on the margins and a wholehearted effort to bring everyone home to the table of the Holy One.

Come Again, Come

Yea, though I walk through the valley of the shadow of death,
I will fear no evil: For thou art with me; Thy rod and thy
staff, they comfort me. Thou preparest a table before me in the
presence of mine enemies; Thou anointest my head with oil;
my cup runneth over.

Psalm 23: 4–5

Come to me, all you that are weary and are carrying heavy
burdens, and I will give you rest.
Take my yoke upon you and learn from me, for I am gentle and
humble in heart, and you will find rest for your souls.
For my yoke is easy and my burden is light.

Matthew 11:28–30

Come, come, whoever you are.
Wanderer, worshipper, lover of leaving—it doesn't matter,

Ours is not a caravan of despair.

Come, even if you have broken your vow a hundred times,

Come, come again, come.

Mevlana Jalaluddin Rumi

MAYBE THE MOST difficult stranger to welcome is the one who lives inside us. For much of my early life, I banished myself to the wilderness of my specialness. I was pretty sure I got the cosmic joke—I knew this world as an illusion, a flimsy screen barely obscuring the Real World just beyond it—but no one else seemed to be laughing. I had dropped down to earth awake, and everyone else seemed to be sleepwalking.

On the other hand, I self-identified as a tragic figure. My personal story was full of sorrow and betrayal, and I left a puddle of tears wherever I went, but most people just stepped around it without a second glance. If they knew what I had been through, they would proclaim me a hero! Instead, I resigned myself to being unrecognized and misunderstood.

Little by little, the tragedies and comedies of the human predicament wore away the veneer of entitlement, and I began to find my place in the messy web of life. I was not the only girl who had fallen for that old trick of the phony guru who claims that by giving him her virginity she will fly straight into the arms of God. I was in good company among the violated and the disillusioned—those who had weathered divorces and poverty, addictions and terminal illnesses, ostracized from a community they helped to build and risking everything for a love that dissolved in their hands. I no longer wore my story like a badge. I peeled off the whole damned uniform and went around naked.

Feed My Sheep

Deeply moved at the sight of his brother, Joseph hurried out and looked for a place to weep. He went into his private room and wept there.

After he had washed his face, he came out and, controlling himself, said, "Serve the food."

. . . .

The men had been seated before him in the order of their ages, from the firstborn to the youngest; and they looked at each other in astonishment. . . . Portions were served to them from Joseph's table. . . . So they feasted and drank freely with him.

Genesis 43:30–31, 33–34

When they had finished eating, Jesus said to Simon Peter, "Simon son of John, do you love me more than these?"

"Yes, Lord," he said, "you know that I love you."

Jesus said, "Feed my lambs."

Again Jesus said, "Simon son of John, do you love me?"

He answered, "Yes, Lord, you know that I love you."

Jesus said, "Take care of my sheep."

The third time he said to him, "Simon son of John, do you love me?"

Peter was hurt because Jesus asked him the third time, "Do
you love me?" He said, "Lord, you know all things; you know
that I love you."
Jesus said, "Feed my sheep."

John 21:15–18

O mankind! Lo! We have created you male and female, and
have made you nations and tribes that ye may know one
another. Lo! the noblest of you, in the sight of Allah, is the best
in conduct. Lo! Allah is Knower, Aware.

Surah al-Hujurat 49:13

TWO EVENTS SERVED as the combined catalyst for the transformation of the young journalist and civil rights activist
Dorothy Day from atheist-anarchist to passionate lover of
the God of Love. First, she was arrested for her involve-
ment in the suffragist movement of the 1920s, and spent
thirty days in jail. During this time, Dorothy experienced a
visceral identification with prisoners whose basic human
rights are violated. Then, she became pregnant out of
wedlock and, having opted for an abortion a few years
earlier, experienced her impending motherhood as radical grace, cleansing her soul and awakening an intense
longing for the Divine. She converted to Catholicism and
dedicated the rest of her life to serving God by serving
the poorest of the poor. This effort became known as the
Catholic Worker Movement, and it flourishes to this day.

IT MAY SEEM obvious to us in the early twenty-first century, standing as we do on the shoulders of the spiritual

activists who came before us, that there is a necessary connection between religious belief and responding to those in need. But Dorothy Day followed this teaching to its core: it's not enough to tend those who suffer from the devastating effects of poverty; we must expose the causes of poverty and eradicate them. We must wake up to our collective humanity and act in accordance with the most radical messages of the Gospel. We must live the Beatitudes with every breath.

> *Blessed are the poor in spirit: for theirs is the kingdom of heaven.*
> *Blessed are they that mourn: for they shall be comforted.*
> *Blessed are the meek: for they shall inherit the earth.*
> *Blessed are they which do hunger and thirst after righteousness:*
> *for they shall be filled.*
> *Blessed are the merciful: for they shall obtain mercy.*
> *Blessed are the pure in heart: for they shall see God.*
> *Blessed are the peacemakers: for they shall be called the children of God.*
> *Blessed are they which are persecuted for righteousness' sake: for theirs is the kingdom of heaven.*
>
> Matthew 5:3–10

MY FRIEND NANCY met Dorothy Day in 1958. At the time, Nancy was a college student in Syracuse. Although she had been born and raised in upstate New York, she had never been to New York City. Daniel Berrigan, then a radical young priest with a developing ministry of social justice, invited Nancy to meet him in the Bowery to visit a remarkable woman who had set up a "hospitality house" during the Depression in the office of her underground newspaper, *The Catholic Worker*. Decades later, this mission had flowered into a network of homes where volunteers offered food to the unemployed and a place to sleep to the homeless.

The young girl traveled alone by train to the city and navigated the subway system to the Catholic Worker house on the Lower East Side, where Dorothy Day still lived and served the destitute. When Nancy knocked at the door, an older woman dressed in shades of brown, her hair coiled in a long gray braid on top of her head, opened the door. A small boy clung to the hem of her housecoat. Dorothy did not smile. She did not even greet her young visitor. Instead, she looked the girl over, as if assessing her usefulness, and without diverting her gaze from Nancy's face, spoke to the child beside her.

"This nice young lady will take you home, and buy you milk and bread on the way." With a kiss on top of his head, Dorothy ushered the child onto the stoop, stepped back inside, and closed the door behind her.

"There was no doubt in my mind that this is exactly what would happen," Nancy says. The child took her hand and guided her to the corner market where Nancy purchased the groceries, and then she followed the boy to a rundown tenement on the corner. When they entered, the apartment was filled with children speaking Spanish. A middle-aged man, who was later identified as the little boy's father, sat in a chair by the window. Both his arms were bandaged from the hand to the elbow, and he had them propped up on the windowsill.

Nancy learned that the man had suffered from an industrial accident and had been out of work for months. Not only had the factory where he worked failed to offer compensation, but they had fired him. He was responsible for the care of several families who lived with him, and Dorothy Day and her team had been helping out during this difficult time. Nancy was welcomed as part of the extended family, and she spent a couple of hours visiting with the members of the little boy's household.

When she made her way back to the Catholic Worker house, Dan Berrigan was waiting for her. He led her into the kitchen where the bottomless pot of soup was simmering on the stove for the evening's meal. Dorothy was sternly lecturing a young priest. "Words are not enough," she said. "You have to do something!" In that moment, Nancy took this message as if it were meant for her, and dedicated her own life to defending human rights and uplifting the human spirit.

There are Dorothy Days everywhere. Some are known; others serve invisibly. None seem to be interested in personal recognition, and dismiss characterizations as saints as silly and irrelevant. Sister Lucy Kurien, a Catholic nun from South India, is such a one. An advocate for battered and destitute women in her country, Sister Lucy and her team have saved the lives of a couple of thousand women and children since she established her first interfaith shelter, called Maher ("Mother's House" in the local dialect), in the late 1990s.

I had the great fortune of meeting Sister Lucy at a recent interspiritual gathering, where we had both been invited to speak about the intersection where love for the Creator meets service to the Creation. The moment we first encountered one another, Lucy greeted me as if I were her long-lost little sister, an attitude, I soon discovered, she adopts with every person who crosses her path.

Sister Lucy struck me as a jovial Mother Teresa. She is unpretentious, speaking her mind and heart with child-like simplicity and laser clarity, and she seems to inspire everyone around her to drop everything and start helping the helpless. There is not a trace of guilt or drudgery in this impulse; Lucy makes selfless service to people of all faiths and every social station an opportunity for pure delight. At Lucy's table, everyone is welcome, cherished, and invited to sing her own special love song to the God of Love.

Sheikh Abdul Aziz Bukhari, co-founder of Jerusalem Peacemakers (with Eliyahu McClean) and the head of the Naqshbandi Sufi order in Jerusalem, dedicated his life to celebrating the interconnectedness between the Children of Abraham. By the time Sheikh Bukhari died of a heart attack in 2010 at the age of sixty-one, his example had rippled through the war-torn heart of Palestine and Israel, offering a viable path through the seemingly un-ending conflict: unconditional love. Jews, Christians, and Muslims continue to gather in the Holy City to perpetuate

Bukhari's legacy of interfaith dialog and interspiritual worship.

The sheikh did not invent this approach. For Bukhari, the unifying teachings at the core of the three monotheistic faiths proclaimed a single message: love one another. He did not, however, minimize the challenge in implementing this. "The stronger one is the one who can absorb the violence and anger from the other and change it to love and understanding," Bukhari said. "It is not easy; it is a lot of work. But this is the real *jihad*."

The price we pay for unlatching the gates of the heart and inviting everyone in for a feast can be higher than we bargained for. Yet, the welcome works both ways: we too find sanctuary among the human family. Even as we offer sustenance, we are fed. It is not required that we dress in a certain way or speak a particular language. We can show up late, unkempt, in a cynical mood, only to discover that the best piece of cake has been saved just for us.

SACRED SERVICE
Compassionate Action

When our learning exceeds our deeds we are like trees whose
branches are many but whose roots are few: the wind comes
and uproots them. . . . But when our deeds exceed our learning
we are like trees whose branches are few but whose roots are
many, so that even if all the winds of the world were to come
and blow against them, they would be unable to move them.

Prayer Book for Shabbat, Talmud

What good is it, my brothers and sisters, if you say you have
faith but do not have works? Can faith save you? If a brother
or sister is naked and lacks daily food, and one of you says to
them, "Go in peace; keep warm and eat your fill," and yet you
do not supply their bodily needs, what good is that? So faith
by itself, if it has no works, is dead.

James 2:14–17

What actions are most excellent? To gladden the heart of
a human being, to feed the hungry, to help the afflicted, to

*lighten the sorrow of the sorrowful, and to remove the wrongs
of the injured.*

Hadith

Love Poems to the Holy One

YOUR HEART IS so drenched in love for the Beloved that
it overflows into everything you do. You are incapable
of making distinctions between the sacred and the pro-
fane: each act has become an act of prayer. When you ask
your mother for a drink of water, you are begging the
Holy One for a glimpse of His face. When she hands you
the cup and you thank her, you are praising the God of
Love for quenching your spiritual yearning. Stirring the
oatmeal, you are preparing an offering for the Divine.
Reorganizing the closet, you are cleansing your heart so
that the Holy One may find refuge in you.

In the past, you strove to be perfect. You kept a list
of tasks you considered to be worthy, and another you
dismissed as selfish. You developed a rating system and
judged yourself according to the results. Now you wash
dishes for God. Now when you dance the tango you are
dancing with the Holy One, when you check email you
are corresponding with the Holy One, and when you
grade papers you are giving encouragement to the Holy
One. Undressing your lover is unwrapping a divine gift;
eating chocolate is partaking of a sacrament. Forgetting
to drop off the recycling, neglecting to call your dad on
his birthday, getting offended when your friend suggests

that your jeans are too tight—these are all comedy routines you perform for the God of Love, which crack Him up and make Him love you all the more.

So perhaps you travel to India to make art with orphans. Not because you are stoking the fires of charity so that you will be safe and warm in the Afterlife. When you squat on the streets of New Delhi with homeless children and spread out the magic markers before them, you see the face of God light up with delight. Maybe you spend your weekends picking up litter on the side of the highway. Not so the Lord will nod His holy head in approval and your neighbors hide their faces in shame for having been such slobs. Even as you stuff fast food wrappers into your ten-gallon lawn-and-leaf bag, you are shampooing and brushing and braiding the hair of the Divine Mother, who sighs and relaxes under your tender touch.

The best are the moments when you so thoroughly lose yourself in serving the One you love that there is nobody there but God. It is the Holy One singing hymns to the Holy One. It is the Absolute bailing the Absolute out of jail. It is the sacred holding the hand of the sacred as she takes her last breaths in the inner city hospital. It is the Ground of Being cultivating the community garden inside herself, and dropping off the excess at the local food pantry. It is the God of Love writing love poems to Himself, and reading them aloud, and giving thanks for such beauty, such generosity, such astonishing grace.

Follow Your Heartbreak

> It is clear that "to serve God" is equivalent to serving "every
> living thing." It is for this that the best among the Jewish
> people, especially the prophets including Jesus, ceaselessly
> battled.
>
> Albert Einstein

> What the Beloved wants from us is action. What he wants is
> that if one of your friends is sick, you take care of her. Don't
> worry about interrupting your devotional practice. Have
> compassion. If she is in pain, you feel it, too. If necessary, you
> fast so that she can eat. This is not a matter of indulging an
> individual; you do it because you know it is your Beloved's
> desire. This is true union with his will.
>
> Teresa of Avila, The Interior Castle

> Feed the hungry and visit the sick, and free the captive, if he
> be unjustly confined. Assist the person oppressed, whether
> Muslim or non-Muslim.
>
> Hadith

ALL THE RELIGIONS of the world seem to hold compassionate action as their highest ideal. Yet the suffering in this
world can be overwhelming. Where do we begin to alleviate the pain that spills like blood down every street of this
life? How do we keep ourselves informed about the issues that plague the people, the animals, and the earth we
all share? How do we make wise choices when it comes to
sharing our limited personal resources?

ANDREW HARVEY, FOUNDER of the Institute for Sacred Activism, acknowledges the magnitude of the challenge to respond with compassion to the vast array of social and environmental crises. When the suffering of the world feels like too much to bear and you cannot figure out where to begin to help, pause and check in with your heart, he says. Find the cause that most deeply moves you—the suffering that most radically breaks through the protective layer of your complacency—and use that as your guide. *Follow your heartbreak*, is the way Harvey puts it. Choose one heartbreaking issue—one broken thing—and dedicate yourself to learning everything you can about it, and then do whatever you can to repair it.

The sacred scriptures offer paradoxical guidance on the moral imperative. In some cases, we are promised that if we do good deeds here on Earth, our reward will be great in heaven. On the other hand, we are encouraged to give of ourselves freely, without any expectation of recognition or compensation, either from God or from our fellow humans.

Selfless service is generally deemed a purer thing than doing good with an ulterior motive. Yet most of us would agree that a little payoff—at least in terms of that feeling of well-being that flushes through our hearts when we serve soup to the hungry or visit a sick friend in the hospital—is a source of motivation to keep giving all we can. It's not supposed to hurt to be generous. We are allowed to harvest the bounty of joy. The trick is to not make personal benefit your primary purpose for acting with compassion.

Rabbi Jesus agreed with Hebrew Scripture that the highest form of giving is to give anonymously. In fact, he was in agreement with most of the Jewish ethical teachings. "I have come not to abolish the Laws of the Prophets," Jesus assured his Jewish followers, "but to fulfill them." And yet, in the tradition of all great Jewish sages, he elaborated on the ancestral wisdom teachings. "When you do your alms," he warned, "do not sound a trumpet before you . . . that you may have the glory of men." Rather, "when you do alms, do not let the left hand know what the right hand is doing." Instead, let "your alms be done in secret, and your Father who sees in secret shall himself reward you openly."

How do we strike a balance between tending to our own welfare and serving the endless needs of humanity and the earth, between pouring ourselves out into the world and seeking to refill our own cup? How do we ensure that we are not rolling down a path of convenience, showing up to serve when it suits our comfort and boosts our prestige, and withholding our gifts when we are feeling impoverished and underappreciated?

This is not a modern dilemma. The biblical prophets had to trumpet their message to wake people up: *How can you sit there in your comfortable homes with the windows and doors shut tight against the suffering of your neighbors?* they bellowed. *Do something now! The fires burning down the street will soon engulf us all.*

Isaiah, Jeremiah, and Micah had a problem with religion based only on worship and ritual, religion empty of the practice of kindness, the expression of mercy, and the commitment to righteousness. Disregard for the Divine commandments between people and their fellow human beings, the prophets agreed, makes a mockery of the commandments between a man and his God. Of the 613 *mitzvot* (commandments) that comprise the *Halakhah* (body of Jewish law), the majority are ethical in nature. The root of the word *mitzvah* is "connection." Righteous action connects us with one another and with our God.

"He has shown you, O mortal, what is good," Micah reminds us: "And what does the Lord require of you? To act justly and to love mercy and to walk humbly with your God" (Micah 6:8). The Talmud lists three attributes as essential for the Children of Israel: mercy, modesty, and generosity. "Now, O Israel," says Deuteronomy 10:12, "what does YHVH, your God, ask of you? Only to fear (be in awe of) YHVH, your God, to go in all his ways." According to rabbinic interpretation, these Divine ways consist in being gracious, compassionate, truthful, and just.

The second-century Talmudic master Rabbi Akiva said that the entire essence of the Torah could be summed up by Leviticus 19:17: "Love your neighbor as yourself." There is a famous story in the Talmud about Rabbi Hillel, another spiritual genius of this lineage. A Gentile came to a rabbi named Shammai and said that he would convert to Judaism if Shammai could teach him the entire Torah while standing on one foot. Infuriated, the rabbi chased the man away. Hillel, however, balanced on one leg and said, "That which is hateful to you, do not do to your neighbor. That is the whole Torah; the rest is commentary. Now go and study it." The Gentile converted on the spot.

While Judaism takes it on faith that the ultimate Divine Being transcends all attributes and defies all description, it also affirms that God is intimately concerned with the human predicament. If human beings are made in God's image and if His nature is one of infinite compassion, then efforts to act with kindness and to defend the persecuted are as vital to spiritual life as are prayer and Torah study. To love God is to love each other and to see each other as having been created in His image, just as we ourselves have been. This is known as "ethical monotheism." Jewish mysticism teaches that the face of God is imprinted on our hearts, and all we have to do is look within in order to know the truth and act accordingly.

Mercy is the root that blossoms into living acts of *chesed* (lovingkindness) and *tzedakah* (righteousness). *Tzedakah* can be confused with charity. But it is not about grand gestures of beneficence. If we are spiritually attuned, giving becomes a natural outflow of our recognition of the interdependence of all life. To withhold what we have from others is to violate the gifts the Holy One has given to us. Not only that, but acts of *tzedakah* are said to sanctify God: our righteousness makes the Holy One holy!

Judaism does not consider humanity to be inherently sinful. On the contrary: according to Abraham Joshua Heschel, Judaism emphasizes "the wonder of creation and man's ability to do God's will" (*God in Search of Man*). Heschel's perspective is that we are never lost: As children of God, we remain active participants in the covenant with the Divine. A *mitzvah*, says Heschel, is not just a commandment we are compelled to obey; it is a prayer expressed as a deed. It is the life of the spirit in action.

Jesus reminded his Jewish followers that the most important of all the Holy One's prescriptions are "to love God with all your heart and all your soul and all your strength" and "to love your neighbor as yourself." Following these two commandments requires a balance between reaching upward toward the divine mystery and manifesting our commitment to the sacred in each other.

In the Sermon on the Mount, Christ calls his disciples "the salt of the earth." By carrying his message of love to all they touch, they will serve to bring out the true flavor of the spiritual life and preserve what is best in the human experience. Sacred service in the name of love, he promises, is worth far more than worldly fame and material fortune. The divine commission is to stand up in our righteousness and radiate our light to the world.

Spiritual gifts, says Paul in 1 Corinthians, are worthless unless they are grounded in love. "If I speak in the tongues of mortals and of angels, but do not have love, I am a noisy gong or a clanging cymbal," Paul writes, paraphrasing the teachings of his Savior. "And if I have prophetic powers, and understand all mysteries and all knowledge, and if I have faith, so as to remove mountains, but do not have love, I am nothing." He praises the virtues of love, charity, and hope, but insists that the greatest of these is love. Paul uses the Greek term *agape* to describe this egoless, sacred, infused love.

From the beginning of his ministry, the Prophet Muhammad emphasized human rights. Islam seeks a balance between individual dignity and a commitment to social equality. In his deathbed sermon Muhammad established the hallmarks of a just and equitable society. "All believers are brothers," he declared. "All have the same rights and the same responsibilities. No one is allowed to take from another what he does not allow him of his own free will. None is higher than the other unless he is higher in virtue."

A hadith of the Prophet teaches that "believers show compassion to one another, have affection for one another, and are kind to one another, as if they were different parts of the same body; if one part ails, the whole body will suffer from sleeplessness and fever." Because Islam considers anyone who affirms the existence of One God as a Muslim, the family of believers includes almost everyone!

Both the Qur'an and the hadiths direct believers to do what is good and refrain from what is evil. The Muslims agree with the Greeks that the gift of reason we have been given by God enables us to distinguish between good and evil. Holiness and beauty are intimately entwined in

Islam: the good is also the beautiful, and that which is evil is ugly.

The root of the word "good" in Arabic is connected to abundance and divine presence. "Evil" is a matter of "wanting" and implies the absence of the Divine. Saving someone's life, then, would be a good act, an act that contributes to the divine abundance, a just act. Killing someone would take away from God that which is His; it would be evil and unjust. This teaching is echoed in the Talmud of Judaism when it says that saving one life is equivalent to saving a universe.

Whether or not our motives are unadulterated, the universal mandate is to disarm our hearts and stretch beyond our comfort zones to respond with love to the cries of the world. Rather than view compassionate action as a penance imposed by a moralistic Father God, we may approach sacred service as a love dance with the Holy One, each move designed to create intimacy and unbounded joy. Instead of concluding that we are too busy and broken to have anything to give anyone else, let us embrace our wounds as evidence of our membership in the human family and allow them to guide us into treating all beings as our mothers and sons, our brothers and grandmothers, doing everything in our power to lift their burdens and bring them solace.

Work

> *Let the beauty of the Lord our God be upon us, and establish*
> *the work of our hands upon us; yes, establish the work of our*
> *hands!*

Psalm 90:17

> *In all things I have shown you that by working hard in this*
> *way we must help the weak and remember the words of the*
> *Lord Jesus, how he himself said, 'It is more blessed to give*
> *than to receive.'"*

Acts 20:35

> *It is not righteousness that you turn your faces towards East*
> *or West; but it is righteousness to believe in Allah and the*
> *Last Day and the Angels and the Book and the Messengers; to*
> *spend of your substance out of love for Him, for your kin, for*
> *orphans, for the needy, for the wayfarer, for those who ask; and*
> *for the ransom of slaves; to be steadfast in prayers and practice*
> *regular charity; to fulfill the contracts which you made; and*
> *to be firm and patient in pain (or suffering) and adversity and*
> *throughout all periods of panic. Such are the people of truth,*
> *the God-fearing.*

Qur'an 2:177

PEOPLE ARE SOMETIMES surprised to discover that I am a
high-school dropout. High school was not a good fit for
me; I couldn't relate to my peers and I felt demeaned by
my teachers. But I loved college. The minute I earned my
proficiency diploma, I began to take classes at the local

community college and didn't stop until I had a couple of degrees. Now I'm a professor of philosophy and world religions, and I love to watch the lights come on in my students as they lit up inside me all those years ago.

When I was sixteen, living on my own in the Pacific Northwest, far from my family in New Mexico, I took a course called Futuristics. It was an interdisciplinary study of sociology, psychology, economics, and philosophy. One of the texts assigned that semester was *Working: People Talk about What They Do All Day and How They Feel about What They Do* by Studs Terkel. What made the most powerful impression on me in Terkel's book was the way certain people approached their job as a sacred mission. Whether they were kindergarten teachers or funeral directors, pipe fitters or fire fighters, these were the people who embraced the opportunity to work skillfully and serve wholeheartedly. I began to romanticize the lives of gas station attendants.

My husband Jeff is a locksmith. He drives around the Southwest installing electronic security systems in hotels. When I have time off from school and he has a job in some beautiful resort or interesting city, I go with him. That's when I drop my persona as a writer and teacher and transform into the lock installer's assistant. I strap on my tool belt, with my cordless drill and my screwdriver collection, and strip the old key locks off the doors so that Jeff can install the card locks. This feeds me at some core level of my being.

For one thing, I love the anonymity of it. In lock world, no one knows that I write books or teach meditation. No one is projecting anything special onto me, hoping I might save their soul. In the beginning, I have to admit, the anonymous part was not quite so refreshing. I recall bending over a doorknob with my power tools, making a lot of noise and kicking up sawdust, my bandana pulling my hair out of my eyes, when a well-dressed woman walked past me without a glance. It was as if I did not exist, as if the workers of this world were in place simply to serve the needs of those who could afford to stay in fancy hotels. I felt as though I had been slapped. My sense of solidarity with manual laborers everywhere only slightly mitigated my indignation.

But as my worldly recognition increased, my delight in my secret locksmith life deepened. Whenever I accompany Jeff on a job, I have profound encounters with strangers. A young waiter, working his way through college as a musical theater major, sits down with me at our table to tell me about the recent production of *The Pirates of Penzance* in which he played a starring role. I ask all the right questions, and he unfolds like a flower, animated and grateful. As we're leaving the restaurant, he hugs me. When I speak to a Latina housekeeper in Spanish, word spreads throughout the immigrant staff that there is a gringa fluent in their native language. Soon they are bringing extra towels to our room, checking to see if there is anything else I might need, inquiring about my mother and father, how many kids I have. The maintenance man stops by in the hallway where I'm working, and ends up telling me about the way they celebrate *Día de los Muertos* in his village back home in Oaxaca.

One summer, Jeff had a job in a depressed mining town in the southern part of New Mexico, near the Mexican border. Half the buildings were boarded up, the Dairy Queen was the main attraction, and the elementary school looked like a minimum security prison from the 1950s. I went with him because we were going to spend a couple of days in the Gila Wilderness on the way home.

We were scheduled to replace the locks in an old motel near the freeway. When we pulled up, I thought there must be a mistake. The property looked abandoned. Tufts of desert grasses shot up among the cracked concrete of the playground, where the swings hung off their hinges and the bouncy ponies had no heads. There was a detached pool house with an enormous, faded sign that read, "COME SWIM WITH US." But when we peered through the yellowed Plexiglass, we saw that the building was piled with broken furniture. The ambient temperature must have been 104 degrees in the shade. The young Indian couple who owned the place were as lackluster as their property.

"Everyone in this town is a lazy drug addict," the wife informed me.

From my years as a devotee of the Indian saint Neem Karoli Baba, I have learned to chant the *Hanuman Chalisa*, a forty-verse hymn in praise of Lord Hanuman, embodiment of loving service to the Divine. I managed to slip this into conversation with the owners, and the woman's sad eyes sparkled for a moment. "Would you like to sing together?" I asked. "Oh yes!" she replied. And so we did, sitting in her tiny kitchen, the smell of vegetable curry and Nag Champa incense infusing the sweltering air.

Later that day, as Jeff and I were returning to the motel from an expedition to the hardware store, we heard yelling in the parking lot. A truck careened around a corner and screeched to a halt. The passenger door flew open and a beautiful young girl wearing short-shorts and way too much makeup tumbled out. The truck sped away, and she screamed obscenities after it. Then she made her way over to a picnic table and began to sob. I watched her in my rearview mirror as she punched in a number on her cell phone. Soon she was screaming at the person on the other end. "Fine! If you don't want to help me, you can just forget you have a daughter! As if you ever cared in the first place!" And she peppered her diatribe with more expletives.

Jeff went back to work and I approached the girl, who sat sniffling, her face tucked into her arms.

"Are you all right?" I asked.

She lifted her head. She looked dazed, as if she could not imagine what I was doing there. Her eyeliner had migrated down to her chin. She was even younger than I had thought. "Yeah." She tried to smile. "Thanks."

"Okay, well, if you need anything, that's my room over there," I said.

The other aspect of my position as assistant installer is that I have long periods of free time while Jeff does most of the work. I use these breaks to write. I headed back to my room and opened my laptop, but I couldn't concentrate. I kept looking out the window. The girl was still there, sitting in the blazing sun. I grabbed a bottle of cold water and took it out to her. She gratefully gulped it.

"Are you hungry?" I asked. "Do you have any food?"

She began to cry again. "There's food in my room, but my boyfriend took the key and I can't get in."

I put my arm around her and led her to our room. I made her a sandwich and she sat at the little round table across from me to eat. That's when I noticed the dark purple bruise under her eye and the black-and-blue marks on her upper arms and thighs. I gasped. She chuckled ruefully and lifted her tank top. Her back was covered in welts. "He kicked me with his cowboy boots," she said. Then her story came tumbling out.

Her name was Coco ("Coco, like Chanel" she said). She was sixteen years old, from Amarillo. She was the first person in her family to graduate from high school (well, to get her GED, she apologized), and had recently been offered a scholarship to the University of Texas because her old teacher had told them how smart she was. She and her boyfriend got in a big fight (they were always fighting, she explained), and he left for a job and she decided the relationship was over. Then she found out she was pregnant, so she came to find him. She wrecked her Camaro on the outskirts of town. The police impounded it because she was driving without a license or insurance, and here she was: stuck at a dilapidated hotel with an angry, violent man-boy, without any money and with no way to get home.

"You're pregnant?" I said.

"Yup." She shrugged. "I guess there goes college."

I let her stay with me until the boyfriend showed up, contrite and reeking of beer. I glared at him and let her go.

In the middle of the night there was a pounding on our door. Jeff jumped up and called out. "Who's there?"

Silence. I pulled on my robe and stood beside him, peering out the window. It was Coco. She was wearing an oversized T-shirt, her arms folded against her chest. I opened the door, took her arm, glanced in both directions, and pulled her inside. "He's trying to kill me," she whispered.

Now it was Jeff's turn. "You are staying here tonight," he said. Between us, Jeff and I had five daughters. He was not about to let this young girl anywhere near a violent man. "I'm a father of girls. I am calling the police."

"No!" Coco yelped. "I mean, not yet. Please." And she collapsed onto a chair.

We pulled off the torn bedspread and set her up on the floor at the foot of our bed with an extra pillow. Clutching her cell phone like a teddy bear, Coco was asleep in minutes. In the morning, she ate two bowls of cereal and chatted about her dreams of becoming a writer. I took her to the impound lot to see what it would take to get her car back, and balked at the fine: three hundred dollars. The woman who ran the yard looked the girl up and down, frowning. Coco looked away.

"Who did this to you?" she asked.

"What?"

"The bruises. Who beat you up?"

"Nobody," Coco said.

"Listen, I'm married to a state trooper," the woman said. "Just say the word and I'll send him after this loser."

"Her boyfriend," I blurted out. "That's why she needs her car. She has to have it fixed and get out of here."

The woman was quiet, considering. She was beautiful, like Coco. We found out later that she was a Cuban sportscaster from Miami, who had married a native New Mexican, leaving behind the life of a TV anchorwoman for ownership of a junkyard in his hometown. I watched a bond between the older woman and the younger unfold before my eyes.

By the end of the day, Coco had a job at the impound lot, answering phones and organizing files, in exchange for the repair and release of her vehicle. And she had a room at the back of the shop to sleep in. It was a nice space, with a cozy couch and a television, plastic flowers in a vase on the coffee table, plus a minifridge and a microwave. The woman gave Coco a gift certificate to the 7-Eleven on the corner. Satisfied that she was safe, we left our waif in the care of the anchorwoman and returned to the motel.

A few days later, we were hiking along the Gila River. "Do you think rattlesnakes come this close to the water?"

I asked Jeff. Just then, we heard the chattering of a rattle. There on the path in front of us was a giant snake, its tail raised, its head poised to strike. We jumped back and stood transfixed by the magnificent creature.

In some Native wisdom traditions, the snake is a representative of the transmutation of poisons. Whenever you receive "snake medicine," whether in a dream or in waking life, it means that something toxic is being transformed into a blessing. I shared this insight with Jeff.

"That's what was happening in Lordsburg," he said. "You gave those people love—the Indian lady, and the girl from Amarillo—and the venom turned into something sweet."

These episodes on the road with Jeff feel as meaningful to me as any accolades I receive standing in front of an audience that has come to hear me speak about the God of Love. Maybe more.

Mary and Martha, Plus a Couple of Colorado Nuns

> *"Martha, Martha," the Lord answered, "you are worried*
> *and upset about many things, but few things are needed—or*
> *indeed only one. Mary has chosen what is better, and it will*
> *not be taken away from her."*
>
> Luke 10:41–42

MARTHA BUSTLES AROUND the kitchen, chopping onions and carrots for the Lord's supper. She steams the rice and pokes the fish. She wipes the stone table for the third time.

Jesus will be here any minute. She wants everything to be perfect for the Son of God.

"Mary!" she calls. "Pick some mint for the lemon water, will you?"

But her sister does not respond. Mary has walked to the well for water and forgotten her errand. She has sat down to watch a pair of swallows taking turns stuffing bugs into the mouths of their fledglings. Mary is in rapture—as usual.

Jesus arrives, silent on bare feet. He touches Mary's shoulder. "My Lord!" she cries, and wraps her arms around his legs, gazing up at him. He touches her hair, reaches for her hand, lifts her to standing.

"What's for dinner?" he asks.

The two friends walk together to the house Mary shares with her older sister, Martha, and their little brother, Lazarus.

When she sees them through the kitchen window, Martha bustles out into the yard, wiping her hands on her apron. "Rabbi!" she calls out.

"My friend!" says Jesus, and he embraces Martha.

"Sit," she commands. "I'll bring wine."

Rabbi Jesus settles onto a bench beneath a cypress and receives the cup from his hostess's hand. "Where is Lazarus?" he asks.

"On his way home," Martha answers. "At least I hope so. I need him to help me bring in wood for the cook fire."

"I'll do it!" says Mary, but the minute her sister disappears back into the kitchen, Mary forgets her offer and folds herself at the rabbi's feet. "Tell me how to hear the voice of God," she says.

"Dissolve into love," says Jesus.

And with that, the two friends fall silent, dissolved.

This is the way Martha finds them a half an hour later.

"Mary!' she says. "Where's my firewood? And you!" she turns to the Christ. "You're distracting her from her work. I need help."

Jesus turns toward her, as if he were coming back from a long inner journey.

"Don't worry, Martha," he says. "I appreciate all you do, but you do not serve me only by filling my bowl with bread and olives. It also makes me happy when you lay down your burdens and sit with me, exploring the Torah, listening to the silence."

Mary and Jesus watch as consternation appears on Martha's face. She is grappling with emotions. The part that surrenders drops the wooden spoon with a clatter. The triumphant part plops down on the bench beside her beloved guest. "Tell me," she says. "How can I hear the voice of God?" She grabs Jesus's hand. "This is all I want, yet there are so many things I feel responsible for. Who else would take care of these chores if I didn't?"

Author Tessa Bielecki, co-founder and former abbess of a Carmelite monastery, cannot fathom why people mark such a rigid distinction between the active and con- templative life. One informs the other, as naturally as the two wings of a bird are both required for flight. In *Holy Daring*, Tessa writes of her spiritual hero, Saint Teresa of

Avila. "She is not only one of the greatest contemplatives in the Western spiritual tradition, but also one of its greatest activists. Tremendously involved with people and projects, constantly on the go, Teresa still found time to make prayer a priority."

Tessa points out that many people use the gospel story of Mary and Martha to set up a false dichotomy between action and contemplation, to justify their "compulsive addiction to work," on the one hand, or their "laziness and inertia," on the other. But what Christ intended, Tessa insists, was not "either/or" but "both–and." We are called to be contemplatives who are passionately engaged in the world, and activists who ground our efforts in the silence and stillness.

A few years ago, I had the great fortune of visiting Jonah House, a Christian-based community of nonviolent resistance in Baltimore. I went to see my friend, Liz McAlister. Liz is the widow of Philip Berrigan, prophet of peace, brother of legendary activist Father Daniel Berrigan. Liz, too, has dedicated her life to upholding and modeling what she considers to be the most essential of all biblical teachings: *Thou shalt not kill*. She has been imprisoned countless times for her acts of civil disobedience, in an ongoing witness to the God of Love. Liz once told me that she and Phil timed their peace actions so that if one of them were arrested, the other one would be home to take care of the children.

My visit to Jonah House coincided with the release of my translation of *The Book of My Life*, Teresa of Avila's autobiography. I was on a speaking tour, in which I was highlighting the social justice aspects of Teresa's teachings in an effort to portray the mystic as a peace activist. This was during a period when I was struggling to reconcile my own contemplative inclinations with my ideas about the need for action.

Located in the heart of inner-city Baltimore, Jonah House nestles at the edge of a turn-of-the-century Irish cemetery. The residents have an agreement with the city to live there in exchange for reclaiming the historic graveyard from the clutches of the southeastern forest that has engulfed it and restoring the ornate tombstones. This is an effort that has spanned many acres and a couple of decades. Most people who visit the house work when they are there. Yet Liz and the other residents embraced me like a long-lost pilgrim and offered me refuge from the demands of traveling and teaching. They set me up in a beautiful private room, drew me a hot bath, and dosed me with aspirin for my sore back. The only chore they allowed me was feeding the goats, which was more about joyful play than any kind of labor.

Jonah House has been a hub for Plowshares actions over four decades. Plowshares actions derive their name from the residents' passion for the scripture from Isaiah, in which the prophet predicts a time when "they will hammer their swords into plowshares and their spears into pruning hooks. Nation will not lift up sword against nation, and never again will they learn war" (Isaiah 2:4).

Among the cast of characters living at Jonah House when I was there were two Dominican nuns, named Ardeth and Carol, who were in their sixties and seventies. Known by the media as "the Colorado Nuns," the sisters had recently been released on parole after spending a year and a half in federal prison for having broken into a nuclear missile silo in Colorado in 2002 and painted crucifixes on the warheads with their own blood. The government called them "terrorists," which might have been funny if it hadn't been so disturbing. "To be labeled a terrorist is really very hard to hear and to accept, when your whole life has been one of loving nonviolence," Ardeth admits.

On my second afternoon at the house, we were all sitting around the living room after the ecumenical Sunday morning service. Carol was knitting and Ardeth was serving oatmeal chocolate-chip cookies. They seemed much more like a couple of Midwestern grandmothers than international criminals. The sisters were taking turns praising my new book, and I tried to receive the compliments graciously, but I began to feel increasingly uncomfortable. Finally, I blurted out, "I feel like a fraud!"

"Why?" Carol asked.

"Why?" Ardeth echoed.

"Because here I am translating long-dead mystics, and there you are risking everything and going to prison, for the teachings of peace. My work is esoteric. Meaningless. What good is it doing anyone?" And, to my further embarrassment, I began to cry. Years of secret guilt had brought me to this moment of confession.

Carol laid down her yarn, tucked the needles into the skein, and gave me her full attention. Ardeth knelt at my feet. Liz, the least sentimental person I know, came in from the kitchen where she had been preparing pasta primavera, sat on the couch beside me, and took my hand in hers. And the three women proceeded to convince me that my work was of vital importance, and that reading translations and reflections by people like me gave people like them the inspiration to do what it is that they do. "It's a circle of reciprocity," one of them said. "We take turns renewing each other along the way," said another.

From that holy moment onward, I have never again felt caught on the horns of a dilemma that sets the hero of action up against the pretender of contemplation. I am no longer conflicted about what I do. My friend Father Bill once described it like this: "The person who gives the prophet a drink of water is serving God just as much as the prophet is." I pray that my books may be a dipper of cool water in this burning world.

MERCY
Forgiveness and Reconciliation

Who is a God like you, who pardons sin and forgives the
transgression of the remnant of his inheritance? You do not
stay angry forever but delight to show mercy. You will again
have compassion on us; you will tread our sins underfoot and
hurl all our iniquities into the depths of the sea.

Micah 7:18–19

But I tell you: Love your enemies and pray for those who
persecute you, that you may be sons of your Father in heaven.
He causes his sun to rise on the evil and the good, and sends
rain on the righteous and the unrighteous.

Matthew 5:44–45

Allah the Almighty has said: "O son of Adam, so long as you
call upon Me and ask of Me, I shall forgive you for what you
have done, and I shall not mind. O son of Adam, were your
sins to reach the clouds of the sky and were you then to ask
forgiveness of Me, I would forgive you. O son of Adam, were

you to come to Me with sins nearly as great as the earth and
were you then to face Me, ascribing no partner to Me, I would
bring you forgiveness nearly as great as its."

Hadith, on the authority of Anas

Grace

MAYBE YOU WERE violated as a child: there is no denying it. It was not your fault; you were too young to defend yourself. You wandered—curious, guileless—into the grizzly's cave and woke him. He ate you up. An adult you trusted betrayed you: plundered your body, shredded your confidence, fractured your spirit. You grew up crooked, thickened around your wound, exposed to the bone in the places where once you were whole. It took you decades to realize that what happened to you was not right, would never be right. This knowledge is more than you can bear. You bear it anyway. You are lovely and brave.

But your fury seethes under the surface of your life like an infestation of termites. From time to time the demons erupt and you find yourself lashing out at your difficult children or your unhelpful lover and you hate yourself, and the one who hurt you—all those years ago—all over again. You try to keep your resentments in a cage in your heart, but they escape. You deal with the damage and lure them back inside. You feed them and they grow. You starve them and they multiply. You are not their jailer after all, but their prisoner.

Then one night you wake up and your heart is quiet. The worst thing that has ever happened to you is curled up, harmless, at your feet. You stroke it, open the door, and wave good-bye as it leaves. You picture the people who hurt you most deeply. They are crying. Overcome with empathy, you too begin to weep. Without any words, you forgive them. Grateful, they disappear, like a genie released from a bottle after the curse is finally lifted. You have never felt such stillness, such a gentle breeze moving through the cells of your body. You fall back to sleep, and rest more comfortably than you can remember since you were a small child, a child who believed the world was a safe and exciting place, managed by grownups who knew what they were doing and loved you unconditionally.

The sages have taught you to love your enemies and forgive those who persecute you, but what they forgot to tell you is that you are powerless to achieve this on your own. You can cultivate a loving heart through prayer and fearless self-inquiry, small acts of kindness, and more radical acts of social justice. You can turn toward your pain and say yes to your life, but you need the God of Love to meet you halfway. You cannot forgive without grace, and grace is not something you can demand. You can only sweep out the chamber of your soul and be ready to receive it when it comes.

And when it does, there is not a doubt in your mind that you have been blessed. No effort of your own could have yielded this lightness of being.

Returning

> *Our rabbis taught: Those who are insulted but do not insult,*
> *hear themselves reviled without answering, act through love*
> *and rejoice in suffering, of them the Scripture teaches, "But*
> *they who love him are as the sun when he goes forth in his*
> *might"* (Judges 5:31).
>
> B. Shabbat 88b, Talmud

> *You have heard that it was said, "Eye for eye, and tooth for*
> *tooth." But I tell you, do not resist an evil person. If anyone*
> *slaps you on the right cheek, turn to them the other cheek also.*
> *And if anyone wants to sue you and take your shirt, hand*
> *over your coat as well. If anyone forces you to go one mile, go*
> *with them two miles. Give to the one who asks you, and do not*
> *turn away from the one who wants to borrow from you.*
>
> Matthew 5:38–42

> *They should rather pardon and overlook. Would you not love*
> *Allah to forgive you? Allah is Ever-Forgiving, Most Merciful.*
>
> Qur'an 24:22

THE HEBREW WORD *teshuvah* has been translated as "repentance," but also as "return." By taking responsibility for our negative actions, we come back into right relationship with our community and with our God. We also return to our true selves as sparks of the Divine, created in the image of the God of Love. A traditional chant from Rosh Hashanah, the Jewish New Year, lures us back to this abiding truth:

Return again, return again,

Return to the land of your soul.

Return to who you are, return to what you are,

Return to where you are born and reborn again.

EACH OF THE three Abrahamic faiths teaches that the moment we approach the Holy One and ask forgiveness for any transgressions against Him, His heart flies toward our heart, lifts us, embraces us, and releases us from blame. They also agree that when we have caused harm to another human being, we must directly apologize to that person and do whatever we can to make amends. Only when we have reconciled with each other can we be right with our God. This requires that we take an honest inventory of our actions and motives, followed by a willingness to face the consequences, change our behavior, and repair any damage we can.

All three faiths set aside a special time each year for the kind of intensive self-reflection that may lead us back home to ourselves. In Judaism it is the High Holidays, beginning with Rosh Hashanah and ending with Yom Kippur (the Day of Atonement), the ten-day period in between known as "the Days of Awe." In Christianity there are the forty days of Lent, leading up to Easter, the Day of Resurrection. In Islam, it is Ramadan, the yearly twenty-nine-day cycle of fasting and prayer that begins with one new moon and ends with the next. In each tradition, these are deeply holy days, infused with reverence, tenderness, and humility.

On Rosh Hashanah, "the birthday of the world," we ask to be "written into the Book of Life" for another year. While some may envision this "book" as some kind of divine ledger that tallies up our right actions in one column and our wrong actions in the other, we can also view it metaphorically and use the High Holiday rituals as an impetus to get back on track with our truest, deepest humanity. Following Rosh Hashanah, we enter a gentle, inward-focused ten-day-period when we are encouraged to spend some time alone and in quietude, reflecting on the year that has passed. We are urged to seek out everyone we feel we may have personally hurt and apologize to them.

Traditionally, we dedicate the twenty-four hours of Yom Kippur to fasting and praying with our community, asking collective forgiveness for our transgressions. The literal translation of the Hebrew word for "sin," *chet*, means "missing the mark." On the Day of Atonement, we endeavor to realign our aim so that we hit life's target with skill and integrity. The liturgy is composed in such a way that, as the sun sets on Yom Kippur, the intensity of our longing for *teshuvah* reaches a crescendo, just as the Gates of Heaven are closing for another year, and we implore the Holy One to assist us in our efforts to return to the path of love.

In the Christian tradition, Lent is the period in the liturgical year between Ash Wednesday and Easter. It commemorates the forty days that Jesus spent fasting and praying in the wilderness, from the moment of his initiation in the River Jordan by John the Baptist to the commencement of his true ministry by the Sea of Galilee. For Christ, this interval was a window of deep contemplation and disciplined self-denial. In the sacred season of Lent, we are invited to follow Christ's example of radical humility, voluntary simplicity, and honest soul-searching.

Lent offers us the chance to let go of habits and modes of being that no longer serve us. Maybe we have found ourselves overly attached to our guilty little pleasures or seriously dependent on harmful substances. Perhaps it is an attitude of cynicism or self-recrimination we wish to shift. Have we been impatient with our children, unappreciative of our spouse, greedy in business, and neglectful of the needs of the more vulnerable members of our community? Lent affords us the space to take a look at where we have strayed from the ideals Jesus modeled, so that we can make amends for any harm and return to the path of love.

Ramadan commemorates the month when the Prophet Muhammad received the first revelations of the Qur'an. For twenty-nine days Muslims fast from daybreak to the rising of the first star in the evening sky. Because the Islamic calendar is lunar rather than solar, the month of Ramadan drifts through all the seasons of the year. This means that some years, when Ramadan falls during winter, the days are short and the fast is gentle. When Ramadan coincides with summer, the fast is more challenging, and requires us to draw more deeply on our inner resources and surrender ever more unconditionally to Allah.

Observing Ramadan is one of the five Pillars of Islam; every Muslim is required to observe the yearly fast. But, as with the notion of a *mitzvah* in Judaism, upholding the Pillars of Islam is more than a commandment; it is a blessing. Muslims look forward to Ramadan all year. While it does involve rigorous purification and self-discipline, Ramadan is also a time of joy, when the *Ummah* (the global Muslim family) joins together to intensify their prayer lives and celebrate their connection to the Divine. The feasts at the end of the day are infused with a quality of sweetness, rooted in sacrifice, empathy, and the felt sense of returning to the path of love.

The unifying theme in each of these faiths is that God loves us unconditionally. Sometimes both practitioners and leaders of the monotheistic religions forget this. We have probably all been guilty of projecting our own unresolved psychological wounds onto Ultimate Reality. The result has been the inadvertent creation of an idol: a small-minded father-god who doesn't trust his children and strikes us down for disobeying his will. But the deeper teaching beneath the surface of the unfortunate image of a wrathful deity is that the Holy One, like a loving mother, meets each of our foibles with tenderness, acceptance, and a desire for us to return to who we really are: children of love. As such, we are given endless opportunities to begin anew.

In Islam, it is said that Allah, who is infinite and transcends all descriptions and forms, nevertheless has ninety-nine names, which evoke His most essential attributes. None of these attributes is "cosmic punisher," or "the vengeful one," or "He who is obsessed with retribution." Rather, Allah has names like *Al-Rahman* (the Merciful) and *Al-Rahim* (the Compassionate). He is called *Al-Ghafur* (the Much-Forgiving) and *Al-Afuw* (the Pardoner). Allah is praised as *Al-Fatah* (the Opener of the Heart) and *Al-Salam* (the Bringer of Peace). A hadith of the Prophet Muhammad expresses the unconditional love of God: Allah says: *"Take one step towards me, I will take ten steps towards you. Walk towards me, I will run towards you"* (Hadith Qudsi).

One of the most beloved of Christ's teachings is the story of the prodigal son (Luke 15:11–32). In this parable, the youngest son of a wealthy man asks his father to give him his inheritance early. The young man pockets his fortune and heads off for foreign lands, where he squanders it all. When famine strikes the country, the young man is forced to take a job feeding swine, an especially onerous task for a Jew. Once he catches himself wishing the pigs would share their swill with him, he recalls that none of his family's servants has ever gone hungry, so he decides to go back home and throw himself on the mercy of his father.

The prodigal son prepares a speech in which he acknowledges his foolish behavior and assures his father that he no longer considers himself worthy to be his child, but that he would gratefully accept work as a manual laborer. The young man does not even have a chance to deliver his declaration, however. When his father sees him coming up the road, he rushes to embrace him, covering his neck with kisses and tears. The father calls for a robe, a ring, and a pair of sandals for his son to wear. He orders the slaughter of a "fatted calf" to be served in a feast celebrating the safe return of his beloved boy.

The older son, at work in his father's fields, hears the commotion and comes to investigate. When he sees his renegade brother being welcomed like a prince, he is furious. He challenges his father, asking why, when he, the responsible one, has toiled all these years for his father and has never been given anything special in return, does the old man throw a party for the one who has "devoured your living with prostitutes."

The father answers, "Son, you are always with me, and all that is mine is yours. But your brother was dead and has come to life. He was lost, and now he is found."

And so the God of Love not only forgives us when we mess up, He welcomes us with a feast when, broken and hungry, we make our way back home.

Fire on the Altar

> *Lord, make me an instrument of your peace: where there is*
> *hatred, let me sow love: where there is injury, pardon; where*

there is doubt, faith; where there is despair, hope; where there is darkness, light; and where there is sadness, joy.

Francis of Assisi

WE CAME TOGETHER in the woods on the shore of Puget Sound: seven spiritual leaders from different faith traditions and several dozen seasoned practitioners. Our purpose was to engage in fearless dialog about the diversity within and the differences between our paths, and to uncover the unifying teachings of love at their common core. Our prayer was to discern how best to be of collective service to the planet and humanity, even as a multitude of global crises threaten to engulf us.

The site for this five-day exploration was a retreat center that had been established forty years earlier, in the mid-1960s, as an interfaith "camp." A Lithuanian rabbi and an Irish Catholic priest had joined together in the spirit of interreligious dialog—an almost revolutionary undertaking in that era. First, they cohosted an interfaith program on Seattle's Challenge TV, which flourished for fourteen years, and then they purchased a beautiful farm with donations from individuals and organizations who shared their vision of a hatred-free zone, where people of all paths could spend time together sharing what is meaningful in their own religion and appreciating the wisdom of other traditions. They called this place Camp Brotherhood.

So the legacy of love was well established by the time we showed up in the summer of 2011. On Friday of that week I was scheduled to lead the group in a sunset

Shabbat ritual. We would sing the traditional Hebrew prayers as we lit the candles, shared a cup of wine, and fed each other pieces of challah in honor of the Jewish Sabbath. That afternoon I spotted the legendary priest who had co-founded the camp walking through the dining hall. We had heard that though in his early nineties, the priest still spent a few hours at the camp most days, and that he enjoyed sharing stories with visitors. So I invited him to join us for Shabbat that evening as our guest, and asked if he would be willing to speak about his and the rabbi's founding vision for a place of interfaith dialog. He was delighted.

Father William Treacy arrived that evening at the chapel, where all our activities were taking place. We gathered in a circle around him like eager kindergarten children while he spun tales of interfaith adventures that had unfolded over the past five decades. Camp Brotherhood co-founder Rabbi Raphael Levine, who was twenty years older than the priest and truly became his elder brother, had died in the 1980s, but Father William said he could still feel his presence permeating his life.

One of the most moving stories Father William told was about the genesis of the altar situated at one end of the chapel, surrounded by windows looking out over the rolling fields and towering pines of the Pacific Northwest. The rabbi's hobby had been woodworking, and his wife was a mosaic artist. In 1964, Father William asked his friend if he would make him an altar for his new parish.

"I was flabbergasted," Rabbi Levine writes in *He Is My Brother: The Bonding of a Priest and a Rabbi Over 25 Years*. "I knew that the altar is the focal point in Catholic worship, the holiest object in the church, and that he should ask me, a Jew and a rabbi, to make an altar for him touched me deeply." The rabbi worked day and night, fashioning an exquisite hardwood altar, inlaid with the ancient Christian symbols of lilies and fish. "Had not the prophet Malachi said, perhaps, 2500 years ago," the rabbi writes, "'Have we not all one Father? Hath not one God created us all? Why then do we deal treacherously, brother against brother?'" The altar was moved to Camp Brotherhood soon after it was made, where it became a symbol of peace between traditions, and the centerpiece for thousands of Eucharist celebrations over the years.

After the priest's talk that Friday, he stood beside me at the altar while I led the Shabbat prayers, participating with a full voice and joyful enthusiasm. The next evening, Father William celebrated Mass for us, using the same candles I had used for Shabbat. The intermingled heart of our traditions was tangible, and it lifted everyone to a state of exaltation.

It was the eve of Pentecost, an incident in the Acts of the Apostles that has always moved me, which commemorates the coming of the Holy Spirit. Many of my Christian friends, having endured certain fundamentalist interpretations which I as a secular Jew have been spared, are not always as enamored of the Pentecost story, but to me it symbolizes the very essence of inter-spiritual understanding.

It is written in Acts that the disciples were gathered in the upper room of a house in Jerusalem during the weeks following the execution of their Lord, hiding from the Roman authorities who sought to persecute them. It was probably *Shavuot*, the Jewish holiday that honors the day the Holy One gave the Torah to the Israelites on Mount Sinai, forty days after their exodus from Egypt. In Christianity, this tradition became absorbed as Pentecost, which was said to have occurred fifty days after Christ's crucifixion.

As the disciples—including Jesus's mother Mary, Mary Magdalene, and other women—sat together in prayer, a rush of wind filled the room. "Divided tongues, as of fire, appeared among them, and a tongue rested on each of them. All of them were filled with the Holy Spirit and began to speak in other languages, as the Spirit gave them ability" (Acts 2:3–5).

Jerusalem was an international crossroads at the time, a sacred pilgrimage site where, between *Pesach* and *Shavuot*, men and women from all nations gathered to worship. As the apostles—newly filled with the Holy Spirit—appeared in the streets, speaking in many tongues, each foreigner found that he could understand exactly what they were saying. All the languages of the world were represented in this miraculous moment. For me, Pentecost is a symbol of reconciliation between faith traditions. It is healing by fire.

During Father William's Mass at Camp Brotherhood that Saturday, he asked me to bring him the Communion wafers—a potent honor for me. After raising the chalice and breaking the Host, the priest explained that he would not be serving Communion to the Catholics present because "until everyone can receive the Eucharist, none of us will." His eyes were moist with tears as he proclaimed his intention, and we all sat in awe of his inclusive heart.

After the ceremony, which many reported was the most beautiful Catholic Mass they had ever witnessed, Sister Lucy led us in a traditional Hindu *aarti* festival to pay homage to Father William, who was turning ninety-two the following day. One by one, we waved a lamp of burning *ghee* in front of the seated priest. Blessed and smiling, he headed for bed.

For our closing devotional practice, I taught the group *Od Yavo Shalom Aleynu* (Peace Will Come Upon Us), a chant in Hebrew and Arabic, which lifted us into an even more ecstatic state. Still singing, we were led outside, down through the woods to a fire circle in a clearing. There we engaged in a Sufi dance, bestowing blessings upon one another. It was a glorious evening.

Until we accidentally lit the altar on fire.

This is what happened while we were dancing. Since we had not been able to find holders for the Shabbat candles the night before, we had improvised, using plastic glasses filled with sand. These were the same candles that had been rekindled on the altar for Mass the next evening. Lost in love, none of us remembered to extinguish the candles before we left the chapel. Fortunately, a couple of people had returned after the dancing to pick up their sweaters, discovered that the altar was on fire, and doused the flames. The organizers spent a sleepless night airing out the chapel and wondering how to break the news to Father William.

I was oblivious to this catastrophe until after the silent meditation and silent breakfast the next day, when we reconvened in the chapel. It was the last day of our gathering. "It's freezing in here," I remarked to Cynthia, the retreat leader, pulling my shawl more tightly around me.

"Oh," she said, "you don't know, do you?"

Cynthia took my arm and led me to the altar at the other side of the room. There on the lower left quadrant of the altar's surface was a small volcano of melted plastic with a black crater at its center.

"We forgot to blow out the candles last night," she said quietly.

I felt as though someone had punched me in the stomach. Having heard the story of how the altar was created and how it had served as the interfaith heart of this place for almost fifty years, I almost could not bear the thought that we had caused such damage.

"It looks like a bomb exploded there, doesn't it?" Cynthia said, and I nodded, mute. In that moment, I understood the way she was seeing this: as a symbol of the violence and woundedness between the Abrahamic faiths, a wound we had gathered here to address, a wound that

Father William and the rabbi had dedicated their lives to healing.

Once our group had reassembled, we raised a thousand dollars in cash for the repair of the altar in a matter of minutes. A beautiful blank card appeared, and we each wrote something in it, offering our apology to Father William. We talked among ourselves for an hour, musing on the symbolism of the scar, the fires of Pentecost, and the danger of allowing altered states of consciousness to lead us into unconsciousness. This event galvanized us as a group so that we faced this experience as one mind and one heart, catapulted into the reality of a community we had hoped to build by our own efforts.

When I returned to New Mexico, I received an email from Cynthia, who had met with the priest after we all left. "He was very gracious, saying that 'accidents happen' and that we should not worry about it any further," she wrote. Father William had lost no time in making the same association we had with the Pentecost and tongues of flame. "He chuckled that we had 'left our mark,'" she continued, "and he reiterated how much he enjoyed our group and said again that it was one of the best groups they've had at Camp Brotherhood."

And so I am reminded that our gravest errors can leave scars that become our most beautiful gifts. And our scars become reminders of grace, of forgiveness. Our wounds can serve as signs of our interconnectedness with all beings, and motivate us to continue striving to make things right between us.

The Doorkeeper and the Dad

The weak can never forgive. Forgiveness is the attribute of the strong.

Mahatma Gandhi

He who takes vengeance or bears a grudge acts like someone who, having cut one hand while handling a knife, avenges himself by stabbing the other hand.

Jerusalem Talmud, Nedarim 9:4

To err is human; to forgive, divine.

Alexander Pope

Forgiveness is not an occasional act: it is an attitude.

Martin Luther King

SISTER JOSEPHINE BAKHITA was born into a royal tribal family in Sudan in 1869, was captured as a slave at age seven, forced to convert to Islam at fourteen, died a Canossian nun in Italy in 1947, and was declared a saint of the Catholic Church in the year 2000. Her life story is a dramatic mix of abuse and healing, martyrdom and reconciliation, faith in the unseen and the pardoning of unspeakable cruelty. Through it all, Sister Bakhita lived the teachings of the Gospels, turning the other cheek each time she was struck in the face, blessing her tormentors with every blow. "If I were to meet the slave-traders who kidnapped me and even those who tortured me, I would kneel and kiss their hands," she said. It was her enslavement that ultimately led her into the arms of Christ.

Between the ages of eight and fifteen, Bakhita was resold five times. The trauma of her abduction drove her original name from her memory, and so she was known by the name her Arab captors called her: Bakhita, which means "lucky." This probably had more to do with their own good fortune in encountering such a jewel of a human being than hers in being so mistreated by people who thought they had a right to own other people. She describes her ordeal with one particularly brutal family.

> *One day I unwittingly made a mistake that incensed the master's son. He became furious, snatched me violently from my hiding place, and began to strike me ferociously with the lash and his feet. Finally he left me half-dead, completely unconscious. Some slaves carried me away and lay me on a straw mat, where I remained for over a month. . . . [Later] a woman skilled in this cruel art [tattooing] came to the general's house . . . our mistress stood behind us, whip in hand. The woman had a dish of white flour, a dish of salt and a razor. When she had made her patterns the woman took the razor and made incisions along the lines. Salt was poured into each of the wounds. My face was spared, but six patterns were designed on my breasts, and 60 more on my belly and arms. I thought I would die, especially when salt was poured in the wounds . . . it was by a miracle of God I didn't die. He had destined me for better things.*
>
> "Saint Josephine Bakhita"

WHEN BAKHITA WAS around sixteen, she convinced her final owner, an Italian diplomat, to take her back to Italy with him when he was forced out of Sudan. Upon disembarking in Genoa, Bakhita was given as a gift to a family friend, and she became a nanny to their baby daughter. At one point her owners took an extended journey to the Red Sea on business, leaving Bakhita and their daughter in the care of the Conossian Sisters near Venice. When the family returned to claim their human possession, Bakhita refused to go with them. The authorities at the convent school advocated on her behalf, the court determined that slavery had been outlawed before Bakhita's birth and that her ownership was therefore illegal, and Bakhita joined the Conossians—the first act of free will in her life. She professed vows in 1896 and was sent to a religious house in northern Italy where she spent most of the next forty-five years until her death.

The young nun embraced religious life with childlike joy and unmitigated humility. No task was too menial for her, and she treated every human being as a long-lost friend. Her primary duty was as the doorkeeper of her convent, which brought her into daily contact with the local community. People were magnetized by her lilting voice and warm smile. They lovingly referred to her as Sor Moretta, (little dark sister) and wanted to know about the events that had brought a traditional African woman to the European continent. The more she told her story, the more she was invited to tell it, and her life became a testimony to the resilience of the human spirit and the willingness of the heart to stay open against all odds.

A more contemporary, but no less astonishing example of this sacred archetype of the wounded healer is my friend, Ted Wiard, an ecumenical minister and grief counselor. As with most of us who have dedicated our lives to serving a particular arena of need, Ted did not randomly choose to minister to the grieving. His path was chosen for him when, over the course of a few short years, he lost almost his entire family.

Ted was the epitome of a "nice guy." Handsome young father of two angelic daughters, married to his high-school sweetheart, he was a skier, a tennis pro, and a middle-school teacher. He made people laugh. His life was uncomplicated, seemingly charmed—until the people he most loved in the world began to die.

First, his brother Richard drowned when the commercial fishing boat he was working on capsized in Alaska. Next, his wife Leslie died of a brain tumor, leaving him with a three-year-old and a five-year-old. Then, when the girls were six and nine, Leslie's mother ran a stop sign with Keri and Amy beside her and collided with a trash truck. All three were killed in the accident. There are other losses that punctuate Ted's story: his first child's unexplained seizure and her mother's subsequent miscarriage; an impulsive second marriage and desperate divorce; a cruel custody battle; a near-fatal illness for Ted (twice); but like rain puddles swept away in a hurricane, the deaths of his children absorbed all other losses.

Ted says of the time following his daughters' fatal wreck and his failed second marriage: "It brought me back into a place of dark introspection and deep depression. My grief process, which included becoming an ordained minister, counseling, reading, a rehab center, time alone, and support from loved ones, allowed me to see light in a tunnel of darkness and reclaim my soul." That's Ted's perspective. For those of us who bore witness to our friend's tragedies, what we saw was a man dragged into the hell realms, plunged into fire, someone who disappeared from our community for a few years and then reemerged shining and more whole than anyone we had ever encountered. Since then, Ted has shown up for the rest of us as we inevitably enter our own wildernesses of grief and loss.

The key to Ted's transformation, I discovered, was forgiveness. He had to come to grips with his feelings about the woman responsible for the death of his daughters—their grandmother, his mother-in-law. At first, Ted says, he could not even acknowledge her existence, let alone her culpability, and least of all her own death. There was no room for Rachel in Ted's heart. If he let her in at all, he would feel he was betraying the memory of his children; if he let himself face the fact that this woman, beloved mother of his late wife, murdered his family, he feared he would unravel completely and never recover from the fury within him. "In my world, she didn't die," Ted says, "because she didn't live. She was simply the driver to my daughters' destinies."

But time passed, as time does, and the state of shock and denial began to wear off. Ted started to consciously engage in the grief process, and in the clarity that ensued, Rachel began to emerge from the ashes of Ted's heart. "I didn't know where to put her," Ted says. "It was complicated. She robbed me of my life, of my children's lives, and of my lineage with Leslie: she could not live on through our children and their children. I wanted to kill Rachel, but she was already dead. Leslie adored her mother. How could I hate her and love her and grieve her all at the same time?"

Forgiveness arose unexpectedly as an outgrowth of the legal proceedings surrounding the accident. Ted's lawyer urged him to file charges against the sanitation worker who was driving three miles an hour over a modest speed limit. Ted refused, imagining that this man was already suffering a life sentence in his own psyche for the deaths of those three people. "I felt this fierce, fatherly protectiveness of the guy," Ted told me. "And in the process of protecting him, my wounded heart began to open, and a seed grew in that space, and the flower was Rachel."

Ted realized that any one of us could have been responsible for the tragedy. Ted had been in the southern part of the state coaching a tennis tournament that day. Maybe if he had been home instead. . . Maybe if Rachel hadn't been facing into the early morning sun. . . Maybe if the driver of the truck had been going just a fraction slower. . . And who among us, Ted asks, hasn't fiddled with the radio knob while driving, rushed to make it across a busy intersection, gotten into the car after a dinner party with a couple of glasses of wine in us? "I thought of all the ways I had driven irresponsibly, lived recklessly, made dumb choices." This process of identification with the flawed family of humanity led Ted to empathy for Rachel, which led to loving her, which led to grieving her, which at last led to forgiving her.

"The final healing took place one day when I realized that I was so glad Rachel had died, so that she would never have to live with what she had done," Ted says. "In that moment, my connection with the person who drove my children to their deaths shifted from my head to my heart, and it has rested there ever since." This is the heart-shift that turned Bakhita into a saint, and Ted into a powerful healer of everybody else's heart.

INDWELLING PRESENCE
The Feminine Face of the Divine

*For she is the brightness of the everlasting light, the unspotted
mirror of the power of God, and the image of his goodness.*

Wisdom 7:26

*Keep her in your mouth, keep her in your heart. Follow the
example of her life and you will obtain the favor of her prayer.
Following her, you will never go astray. Asking her help, you
will never despair. Keeping her in your thoughts, you will
never wander away. With her hand in yours, you will never
stumble. With her protecting you, you will never be afraid.
With her leading you, you will never tire. Her kindness will
see you through to the end.*

Bernard of Clairvaux, "Mary, Star of the Sea"

Woman is the radiance of God, she is not your beloved.
She is the Creator — you could say that she is not created.

Mevlana Jalaluddin Rumi, *Masnavi* I:2437

Made in the Image of God

YOU HAVE BEEN WONDERING: If we are made in the image of God, why doesn't the bearded white Father-God on the ceiling of the Sistine Chapel, breathing life into the first man, Adam, look anything like you? This stern elderly gentleman, draped in expensive robes, lives in the sky. Maybe you are brown skinned and full breasted, which you accentuate with plunging tank tops embroidered with the Harley Davidson logo. Your fingernails are dirty from May through October from planting and harvesting corn, beans, and squash. You are rooted to this earth. Maybe you are a woman who loves women or a man who loves men.

The God of Genesis punishes His children for wanting to know too much. You may get annoyed from time to time with all the questions your kids ask while you're trying to carry in the groceries, check your email, and get a pot of water on to boil for spaghetti, all at the same time: "Mommy, why do dogs pant when they're hot? Why can't we eat cupcakes for dinner? Why do I have to make my bed when I'm just going to sleep in it again tonight? Mommy, why do grandmas die?" But you could not imagine inflicting pain as a penalty for curiosity, let alone for more serious offenses. *Much* more serious offenses. No way.

Your God does not turn away when you are enraged and does not ridicule you when your feelings get hurt. Your God is comfortable with inconsistency. There is nowhere your God is not, and nothing you could ever do to make your God give up on you.

Your God transcends gender. And yet She is also Mother. She is *Shekhinah*, pillar of holy fire, guiding you through the wilderness. She is *Sophia* and *Al-Hakim*, the essence of Wisdom, filling your troubled heart and telling you exactly what needs to be done next. She is *Jamal*, beauty, and *Sakina*, serenity. She is *Rahim*, the merciful source of all life. She is *Shakti*, coursing through your veins when you cry out for God, infusing you with unbearable longing. She is Guanyin, radiating well-being. She is Tara, formed from the Buddha's own tears as he gazed upon the suffering of the world and wept. She is Miriam, Mary, Maryam.

You feel Her closest when you are shattered and when you are exalted. She dives into the heart of the tidal wave and scoops you into Her arms, promising that no matter how disastrous the disaster, She will always be with you. She is in the front row clapping too loudly when you get it right. Your God sneaks you in the back door to *daven* with the learned men in the synagogue. She whispers in your ear when you are trying to control yourself: *Go ahead*, She says, *break the alabaster jar and cover His feet with priceless nard*.

Your God transcends form. And yet She also dwells within every created thing. She animates all that is growing and going to seed, all that is ripened and fragrant, all that is raw and undomesticated. She dwells in creativity, in beauty, in chaos. She breathes with the laboring female animals, breathes with the newborn's first inhalation, breathes with the old ones as they exhale one last time. She is the passion of lovers, the dignity of the queen. She is merciful, but She is not the least bit sentimental.

You do not mean to break the rules and call Her God. You try not to even conceive of God that way. But sometimes you can't help it. Everything that feels holy feels like Her.

Reunifying the Godhead

Does not wisdom call out?
Does not understanding raise her voice?
At the highest point along the way,
where the paths meet, she takes her stand;
beside the gate leading into the city,
at the entrance, she cries aloud:
"To you, O people, I call out;
I raise my voice to all mankind.
You who are simple, gain prudence;
you who are foolish, set your hearts on it.
Listen, for I have trustworthy things to say;
I open my lips to speak what is right.
My mouth speaks what is true,
for my lips detest wickedness.
All the words of my mouth are just;
none of them is crooked or perverse.
To the discerning all of them are right;
they are upright to those who have found knowledge.

Choose my instruction instead of silver,

knowledge rather than choice gold,

for wisdom is more precious than rubies,

and nothing you desire can compare with her . . .

Proverbs 1:11

MOST RELIGIONS RECOGNIZE the Godhead as ultimately one, and yet somehow divided from itself. The masculine has been severed from the feminine, and the two elements seek to return to their essential oneness. This disconnection is mirrored in the human soul, and is responsible for the nameless longing that rises in our hearts in the dark of the night.

While it is true that Western civilization has been skewed toward the patriarchy, a dramatic swing to emphasize the matriarchy might only reinforce the separation. We need to mend the frayed ends of the divine rope, integrating the gifts inherent in both aspects of the divine whole. At the heart of the world's wisdom traditions are vital teachings about how to resolve this false dichotomy.

When the Israelites wandered through the Sinai wilderness, fleeing persecution in Egypt and seeking liberation in Canaan, it was the *Shekhinah* that led them. "By day the LORD went ahead of them in a pillar of cloud to guide them on their way and by night in a pillar of fire to give them light, so that they could travel by day or night" (Exodus 13:21). She dwelled in the holy tabernacle, the Ark of the covenant, covering and protecting the Torah, and she rested in the innermost sanctum of the Temple in Jerusalem once the Israelites had safely settled in the Promised Land.

The holiest day in Jewish life is the Shabbat, and it happens every week. As the sun goes down on Friday, the *Shekhinah* enters, infusing us with a second soul—an additional spiritual resource—to intensify our inner life. The *Shekhinah* exudes a quality of rest and renewal, of awe and wonder, of prayerfulness and celebration. We greet her as a cherished queen, welcome her with honor and delight, and as the sun begins to set on Saturday it breaks our hearts to let her go. Our time with the *Shekhinah* is a taste of *Olam Ha-Ba*, the World-to-Come.

That is why the sages created a special ritual to close the temple-in-time that is Shabbat. During the prayer of *Havdalah* (separation) on Saturday evening, we inhale the fragrance from a box of sweet-smelling spices to keep from fainting with grief that Shabbat is over. It is said that the Blessed One, in His infinite mercy, gives us twenty-five hours of Shabbat instead of twenty-four so that we can spend an extra hour with our beloved *Shekhinah*.

If the *Shekhinah* is the Queen, she is also the Bride. She is the Divine Feminine exiled from the Divine Masculine. She is the Lover the Beloved longs for. When Lover and Beloved are reunited in love, the sacred balance is restored. The contemporary Jewish Renewal Movement, founded by Reb Zalman Schacter-Shalomi, has made tremendous contributions to the interspiritual community by reinvesting the *Shekhinah* with the authority She lost during centuries of patriarchal dominance. Now people of all faiths are turning to the *Shekhinah*, the indwelling presence of the Divine, in the effort to cultivate a more balanced spirituality, one that includes the wild and merciful feminine face of God.

What is it in the psyche of the human family that now so deeply yearns for the Divine Feminine? Why has She been shunned, ridiculed, and buried alive for millennia? Perhaps by revitalizing our relationship with the Holy She, in the form of Mother, of Lover, of most intimate female Friend, we may unfold the treasure map that leads to the resources we need to heal the ravaged planet and all who dwell on her. Tribal peoples have always understood the sacred nature of Mother Earth, but the technological world, in losing its connection with the land, has lost its connection to the Feminine. It's time to reclaim our birthright.

In the Judeo-Christian tradition, the Divine Feminine has been praised in the form of Wisdom, and she was once considered co-creator of the universe. In Proverbs 8, Wisdom says that she was at play with the Lord when He made the All That Is: "Then I was constantly at his side. I was filled with delight day after day, rejoicing always in his presence, rejoicing in his whole world and delighting in mankind." Within Christianity, Holy Wisdom is known by her Greek name, Sophia. The Eastern Church reveres Sophia as an essential component of the Godhead.

According to biblical literature, wisdom is the highest virtue. And yet she is generally ignored, to our great peril. As keeper of the jewels that guide us on the path of righteousness, Sophia imparts divine compassion and invites our participation in cosmic justice. She is the embodiment of sanity and the antidote to the poison of war and violence. The human heart hungers for her, at the same time that the human shadow resists her grace.

Hildegard nurtured a special devotion to Sophia. In Hildegard's cosmology, Sophia held a coequal place with God-the-Father in creating and sustaining the cosmos, a venture rooted in divine passion. "Oh Mother Wisdom," Hildegard cries out, "so greatly does God delight in you, so enthralled is God with you, that He has sunk deep within you the fire of true love, and your body, complete with ecstasy, resounds with the full symphony of heaven." For Hildegard, Holy Wisdom was intimately entwined with Mother Mary.

In the Catholic tradition, Mary is the embodiment of the unconditionally loving mother. Christian theology makes it clear that Mother Mary is not herself divine, but rather a gateway to God, which eternally swings open. She is considered a perfected human being and a model for how to live a loving life. Over centuries of male dominance, the Church has tried to reduce this radiant being to a figure of mild obedience, but the true Marian spirit breaks through any efforts to contain her.

Mary was anything but meek. In spite of the obvious terror the fourteen-year-old child must have experienced as the Angel Gabriel stole into her room at night to announce that she was about to conceive and give birth to the Prince of Peace, Mary gave her unconditional assent.

She nurtured her holy child through every trial, culminating in His agony on the cross. After His death, Mary dedicated her life to upholding and illumining His teachings of love.

Islam also holds an array of powerful women in highest esteem, including Mary of Nazareth. Contrary to the Western stereotypes of Islam as a tradition characterized by the disparagement of the feminine—a misconception due to cultural distortions rather than doctrinal realities—Islam revolutionized sixth-century Arabian culture by liberating women from the status of chattel and affirming their innate intimacy with God. "Paradise," the Prophet Muhammad said in a hadith, "is at the feet of the Mother."

Muhammad's first wife, Khadija, was his employer before she was his spouse. Fifteen years his senior, Khadija was a powerful businesswoman, respected throughout the region. Muhammad and Khadija's daughter, Fatimah, is revered as a perfect Muslim. Muhammad himself constantly praised her spiritual gifts, and some people speculate that the Prophet, who (problematically) did not name a successor before he died, intended Fatimah to continue his spiritual transmission. The Prophet's respect for his daughter was so profound that he often consulted her on both political and religious matters. For many Muslims, Fatimah represents Sophia, the quality of Holy Wisdom. "Allah, the Most High, is pleased when Fatimah is pleased," Muhammad said. "He is angered, whenever Fatimah is angered!"

There are more references to Maryam (Mother Mary) in the Qur'an than there are in the New Testament. An entire chapter is dedicated to her. The Prophet Muhammad described Maryam as the best human being who ever lived. The Qur'an makes it clear that Maryam was blessed from earliest childhood: "Her Lord accepted her a gracious acceptance, and brought her up a gracious upbringing, under the guardianship of Zechariah. Whenever Zechariah entered her sanctuary he found provisions with her. He would ask, 'Mary, where did you get this from?' She would say, 'It is from GOD. GOD provides for whomever He chooses, without limits.' When the angel Gabriel appeared to announce the impending birth of the Prophet Jesus, he cried, 'Behold! The angels said, "Oh Mary! God has chosen you and purified you, chosen you above the women of all nations" (3:42–43). Allah then says, 'And (remember) she who guarded her chastity. We breathed into her of Our spirit, and We made her and her son a sign for all peoples'" (21:91).

Mystically inclined Christians and Muslims tend to be less interested in Mary's physical chastity than her spiritual purity. Mary lived a life of integrity. Her devotion to the Holy One was undiluted by self-interest and unencumbered by dogma. She was neither ethereal nor sanctimonious. She was a protective mother, a proud mother, a worried mother, and a grieving mother. Ultimately, in the hearts of millions who love her, Mary revealed herself as mother of everyone, everywhere, regardless of faith tradition. The Church may revere her as the Queen of Heaven, but she is also adored by the masses as champion of the earth and exemplar of universal responsibility to those who live on the margins.

The Mother Is My Sister

I WAS RAISED by a feminist mother in a progressive, counterculture community, so I have not suffered as much as most of my contemporaries from the sexism and objectification of women endemic in society at large. It was not only my mother who was a feminist. Without preaching any particular sociopolitical position, my father too championed women's rights, advocated for women's power, and venerated women's wisdom. Most of the men and women I knew shared these values. I grew up never questioning my own authority as a woman, nor my equal access to the sacred.

Yet even in my insulated world, certain messages filtered through. In my twenties I bought into the trend of young overachiever Western women and tried starving myself, hoping to transform my naturally curvy body into the shape of an adolescent boy. I kept falling in love with men in positions of authority, in which the power differential made me vulnerable to manipulation. I earned a graduate degree in philosophy, an academic field traditionally dominated by white males, where the few women who were successful seemed compelled to forgo their femininity in order to compete with their male counterparts. I knew something was wrong with all this, but my only hope was an innate impulse to be true to myself, both as a woman and as a human being.

This commitment to self-honoring does not preclude behaving with courtesy when I am a guest in a world that is different from my own. Whenever I attend a Muslim or Orthodox Jewish gathering, I wear a headscarf. My hosts are sometimes surprised and invariably mention that this gesture is unnecessary, yet seem pleased. The truth is, I feel beautiful when I cover my head in this way. I am energized by my sense of solidarity with my Jewish and Muslim sisters. Once, when I was getting ready to attend a Chasidic bar mitzvah, I looked in the mirror and barely recognized my own reflection. Framed by my silk scarf, my face looked harsh to me. No amount of mascara and eyeliner served to soften the image. And yet, when I looked deeper, I seemed to see my true self looking back. It was as if I had come face to face with my own Eastern European heritage, and glimpsed generations of Jewish ancestors blessing me from the mirror.

My friend Latifa, an American convert to Islam, describes what a blessing it is for her to wear the *hijab*. For Latifa, and for many other Muslim women, the head covering is not a symbol of oppression. On the contrary, they feel liberated from the mainstream cultural emphasis on women as sex objects, driven by society to look a certain way in order to be affirmed, and invariably failing to meet the illusory standards of "beauty" imposed upon us. These religious women draw their self-esteem from the beauty of their relationship with God. Secular versions of attractiveness disappear in that radiance.

Sometimes the masculine paradigm can be a doorway to the sacred feminine. Here in the Sangre de Cristos, the southern region of the Rocky Mountain range where I live, an ancient religious brotherhood called Los Hermanos Penitentes (the Penitente Brotherhood) has survived intact for over four hundred years. Because of the remote topography of these high desert valleys, the sixteenth-century Catholic Church could not provide priests for all the outlying communities of Spanish settlers. As a result, the people had to take responsibility for their own religious life. Drawing on medieval religious pageants from the old country, local communities developed a series of rituals that primarily centered on the Passion of Christ, and especially focused on the sacred time between Good Friday and Easter.

Until recently, the activities of the brotherhood were secret. Outsiders were not welcome to either participate in or observe Penitente rituals, and as a result a multitude of misunderstandings and superstitious tales surrounded their activities. Thanks in part to the efforts of *hermanos* like my friend Larry, who is also a historian, the beauty of the *hermanidad* is now beginning to be accessible to nonmembers. For the past few years on Good Friday, Larry has extended an opportunity for visitors to respectfully observe an essential Penitente rite: *el Encuentro* (the Encounter). Not long after my daughter was killed in a car accident, Larry invited me to *el Encuentro*, and this experience became one of the most healing moments of my harrowing journey through grief.

Here's how the Mother helped mend my heart:

We are invited to gather at noon on Good Friday in the dirt parking lot outside the Holy Trinity Church in a small village at the foot of a mountain. Across the road, nestled among the willows, is the *morada*, the low, windowless adobe building where most of the private Penitente ceremonies take place. *Los hermanos* divide into two groups, accompanied by their wives and *las Verónicas*, the young women dressed in black who represent the girl who brazenly tore off her veil and wiped the sweat and blood from Jesus's face as he labored under the weight of his own gallows up Golgotha Hill.

One group lifts a hand-carved statue of Christ from its casket in the *morada* where he lies all during the rest of the year, sets it on their shoulders, and begins to walk toward the church, chanting the ancient Spanish liturgy in voices fueled by religious emotion. The other group takes *la Madre Maria* down from her altar in the church and moves with her slowly toward the oncoming *hermanos* who are carrying her Holy Son, *Jesucristo*, and singing their own sacred songs. Jesus and Mary will "encounter" one other in the parking lot.

As the two groups approach one other, the cacophony of separate prayers reaches a crescendo. *Hermanos* are weeping as they call out to Jesus and Mary, urging them to be strong in the face of such terrible persecution and suffering. The minor key of the chanting, the booming bass, the two different melodies and rhythms, and the sorrow of the Penitentes, all meet in an explosion of energy as the leader of one procession meets the leader of the other and gently tilts Jesus down to rest against Mary's shoulder.

But they do not linger. "Go away from here, Mother," Christ cries out, through the chanting voices of the *herma-nos*. "I do not want you to see me like this!" And the man carrying Jesus pulls him away. The man carrying Mary pulls her away. The blended procession divides again, and each group walks slowly backward, chanting and weeping, and *el Encuentro* is over.

I drop to my knees in the parking lot. No one could understand my pain like Mary could. She too was a Jewish mother who loved her child beyond all description. She too came face to face with her child's suffering, death, and her own shattering. In this moment, I spontaneously reach out to Mother Mary, pouring my anguish into her open hands, lamenting, consoling, and thanking her all at once. She receives me with quiet yet unmistakable mercy.

Since my own private *encuentro* with Mother Mary, I have never again felt quite so alone in my loss. I still grieve, but she shares my pain, and that makes my burden lighter.

The Motherhood of God

BY THE TIME medieval English mystic Dame Julian of Norwich enclosed herself as an anchoress in a tiny sealed dwelling adjoining a church and dedicated herself entirely to prayer, she had lived through three rounds of the plague, a legacy of violence from the Hundred Years War, and lingering tensions from the Great Schism between the Roman Catholic and Eastern Orthodox Churches. In a world marked by suffering and anxiety, Julian's philosophy of life was revolutionary: "All will be well and all will be well and every kind of thing shall be well."

Julian of Norwich was born in 1342, and we know only one thing about her early life: at some point she asked God to grant her three graces: to bear witness to the Passion of Christ; to endure a life-threatening illness; and to experience the triple wound of contrition, compassion, and longing for God. Soliciting these sacred wounds meant that Julian was willing to follow in the footsteps of her Lord and personally make amends for the errors of the human family, feel the world's sorrow in every cell of her own being, and be ignited with an unquenchable thirst for union with the Divine.

Julian saw Christ as the embodiment of the Divine Feminine. Who else but a woman would bear the pain of the ones she loves inside her own body? "And thus in our creation God Almighty is our natural father," she says, "and God all-wisdom is our natural mother." Like a loving mother, Christ poured himself out for us. "[He is our] natural mother, our gracious mother, because he willed to become our mother in everything, took the ground for his work most humbly and most mildly in the maiden's womb. . . . Our high God, the sovereign wisdom of all, arrayed himself in this low place and made himself entirely ready in our poor flesh in order to do the service and the office of motherhood himself in all things."

When she was thirty, Julian received the first answer to her prayer: she contracted a fever so severe that her priest set a cross before her and administered last rites. She was barely breathing, her sight was failing, and she could feel her soul slipping away from her body. Through her half-closed eyes Julian could see nothing but the crucifix. As she gazed on her suffering Lord, he came alive to her. Suddenly, her own pain disappeared, and she became transfixed by Christ.

Our postmodern, secular sensibilities might cause us to turn away from Julian's descriptions of what happened next. But if we did, we would miss the heart of her entire theology of God's loving kindness. Julian watched as blood began to flow from the wounds where the crown of thorns pierced Christ's head. "The copiousness resembled drops of water which fall from the eaves of a house after a great shower of rain, falling so thick that no human ingenuity can count them." They covered the floor of her cell and splashed up the walls; she expected the blood to soak her sheets. In typical earthy fashion, Julian compares these drops of blood to "herring's scales," like the roof design of the houses all over Norwich. "This vision was living and vivid and hideous and fearful and sweet and lovely."

Sweet and lovely? Blood pouring down the tortured face of her Beloved? This was the first of Julian's sixteen "showings," revelations that unfolded over the course of

her illness. But Julian's accounts of these visions overflow
with appreciation for Christ's "courtesy and friendliness."
She can hardly believe that the Lord of Lords would show
up on her doorstep and offer himself so fully.

The only conclusion Julian can draw from Christ's incarnation, crucifixion, and resurrection is that the One we
so desperately long for longs for us with equal intensity.
"I am the ground of your beseeching," God tells Julian. In
our very turning toward the Divine, the Divine enfolds
us in love. Our suffering and the suffering of Christ are
reciprocal and mutually redemptive. In sacrificing his
own body for our salvation, he becomes the womb of the
world, giving birth to all that is. The Mother and the Son
are one. God is God-the-Mother.

As soon as Julian was well enough to sit up and write,
she recorded her visions in detail. Over time, the significance of Julian's showings ripened. Two decades later, she
wrote about them again, this time weaving in new strands
of understanding. "What do you wish to know of your
Lord's meaning in this thing?" she asked herself. The answer: "Know it well, love was his meaning. Who reveals it
to you? Love. What did he reveal to you? Love. Why does
he reveal it to you? For love. Remain in this and you will
know more of the same. But you will never know different, without end."

STILL SMALL VOICE
Contemplative Life

Be still and know that I am God.

Psalm 46:10

*When you want to pray, go to your inner room, close the door,
and pray to your Father in secret. And your Father who sees
in secret will reward you.*

Matthew 6:6

Call on your Lord humbly and in secret.

Qur'an 7:55

Speaking of Silence

YOU KNOW THAT Ultimate Reality is ineffable, and yet
you cannot help yourself: The unsayable is all you can
talk about. Through poetry and watercolor, dance and
lovemaking, bread you knead and set to rise on top of
the warm stove, everything you do and say, everything

you are, is an effort to tell what happened to you when at the heart of your deepest aloneness the Holy One seeped through the torn fabric of your heart and filled you with love. You cannot say: "I was broken, and God mended me." That is not the true thing.

The true thing happened in a place beyond language, and so you write about gardens, paint shapes and colors resembling nothing of this world, turn up the music and dance like a *dakini* all alone when the children are at school. You run your fingers through your lover's hair. You pour the wine and hand the cups around. You point your finger toward the moon and pray that whoever's looking looks up.

You meet your God in silence. In silence, your God speaks to you, and you understand the primordial language, and it resolves every quandary. This is why you thirst for the silence like a man hiking in the desert who has drunk the last drop in the bottle and does not know how long it will take to reach his car. This is why sometimes you race to your meditation cushion like a mother reunited with her child, and light a candle, drop your gaze, and sink into the embrace of silence. This is why you are not afraid of emptiness: It overflows with gracious plenitude. The God of Love lives here.

It's not always that easy, of course. More often you drag your body to the altar. You feel like a dog banished outdoors when you were just making yourself comfortable on the couch. You sit, you bow, you close your eyes, and then the circus begins. A thousand thoughts, dressed like clowns, come tumbling out of the tiny car of your mind and begin performing their tricks: *I hope those shoes I saw at the mall are still on sale. I think she thinks I think I'm special, but I don't. I think I'm a fraud. I could make burritos for dinner or just broil some fish. I wonder if it's dangerous to eat fish, because of all the mercury. My knee hurts. My knee still hurts. I may have torn a ligament in yoga class. It will take months to heal. This is a disaster.*

People try to assure you that all this mental activity is normal. The great sages speak of the monkey mind: It chases every banana of thought that pops up, giving you no rest. They say the mind is a wild horse that takes off with you, while you hang on for your life. They tell you not to worry about it, to let the mind do what it was made to do: think thoughts. They encourage you to sit down anyway, be still, show up. The trick, they say, is to allow whatever arises to arise, but not to identify with it. Let your thoughts be passing clouds in the blue sky of consciousness. Watch them come, watch them go, don't attach.

Ha! You scoff. *That's for regular people,* you say. *You don't know how bad I am. I've been meditating for decades and it doesn't get any better. I have no discipline. I can't stay focused. I cannot quiet this mind of mine. It's hopeless.*

Maybe it's not hopeless. Maybe when you carve out this sacred time to be still, to be quiet, you are doing all that needs to be done. Maybe, if you reflect on it, there really are moments of grace in between the moments of agitation, and if you were to string these together you would have a strand of contemplative jewels that make your life richer, deeper. Maybe there are longer spaces between the thoughts these days than there used to be. Spaces in which you lose yourself, taste the Absolute, rest in emptiness.

Besides, you are not cultivating stillness for yourself alone. When you drop down into the silence, you lift up the whole world.

The Prayer of Quiet

> *The higher goal of spiritual living is not to amass a wealth of information, but to face sacred moments.*
>
> Abraham Joshua Heschel, *The Sabbath*

> *Remember: if you want to make progress on the path and ascend to the places you have longed for, the important thing is not to think much but to love much, and so to do whatever best awakens you to love.*
>
> Teresa of Avila, *The Interior Castle*

> *The true man of God sits in the midst of his fellow-men, and rises and eats and sleeps and marries and buys and sells and gives and takes in the bazaars and spends the days with other people, and yet never forgets God even for a single moment.*
>
> Ibn Abi'l Khar

DURING THE MIDDLE PART of the last century, many Westerners abandoned the Abrahamic faiths in search of contemplative states in Eastern practices. Now many of us are finding our way back, discovering that these teachings have been at the root of our own heritage all along. In Judaism, the contemplative tradition is emphasized in the study of Kabbalah and woven into the weekly observance of Shabbat. In Christianity, it takes the form of cultivating a personal relationship with the Divine through silent prayer. In Islam, the daily practice of *salat* (ritual prayer) and the continuous repetition of God's name, *dhikr*, evoke inner stillness. Each of these paths requires that we set aside special time to cease from doing and allow ourselves to simply be—alone with the Beloved.

This "sanctification of time," as Abraham Joshua Heschel calls it, is the focus of the Jewish Sabbath. "Six days a week we live under the tyranny of things of space," Heschel says. "On the Sabbath we try to become attuned to holiness in time. It is a day in which we . . . turn from the results of creation to the mystery of creation, from the world of creation to the creation of the world."

How do we accomplish this turning? We pause from our efforts to make things work and remember that we are wondrously made. We set down what Heschel refers to as "the instruments which have been so easily turned into weapons of destruction," refrain from participation in the machine of consumerism, and disengage from "the economic struggle with our fellow man." Most importantly, we stop letting ourselves be driven by our compulsions and dedicate ourselves to spending one day as mindfully as possible. In this way, the Sabbath becomes a radical act, a day of self-governance and freedom. Its most revolutionary fruit is the peace that ripens inside us when we slow down and make ourselves available to the sacred.

Contemplative vocabulary varies from East to West. In Buddhism and Hinduism, the term "meditation" generally evokes a practice of quieting and even emptying the mind of thought. In the Judeo-Christian traditions, meditation practices involve focusing the mind on a specific object of prayer and thinking deeply about it. A Jew might wrap herself up in her *tallit* (prayer shawl) and meditate on a particular psalm, allowing herself to savor and ponder the nuances of the scripture. A Christian might meditate on the Passion of Christ, imagining Jesus's agonized prayer in the Garden of Gethsemane the night before his arrest, seeking to become so deeply absorbed in this event that he is able to identify with and ultimately share in the suffering of his Lord.

The term "contemplation" in Western religious vocabulary is a closer equivalent to what is known as "meditation" in the East. Other names for this practice are "contemplative prayer," "interior prayer," and "mental prayer." The Christian contemplative tradition involves letting go of prescribed prayers and theology, and clearing a quiet space in the heart for God to enter.

In recent years, Father Thomas Keating and other Christian teachers have developed a method called Centering Prayer, which draws on the practice of *zazen* in the Buddhist tradition, blending it with the long-standing tradition of Christian contemplative prayer. Westerners have embraced this practice in vast numbers. In Centering Prayer, we choose a sacred word or phrase as the touchstone of our practice. We sit quietly, drawing our attention inward, seeking to simply abide with the Divine. When we feel our thoughts begin to wander from the present moment, we gently return to the sacred word or phrase and remember that this is our time to rest in our togetherness with the Beloved.

The monotheistic versions of contemplative practice involve a deeper degree of connection to the sacred than that which arises from thinking deeply, or "meditating" about a holy subject. Contemplative prayer is a state of profound quietude. While a practitioner can attempt to cultivate contemplative awareness, it is considered to be a matter of grace when, out of the stillness, the Divine Presence reveals itself. This peaceful companionship with God transcends both sense and intellect: it doesn't carry the familiar emotional content of ordinary awareness and it eludes language, yet it can be the most gratifying and revelatory state the soul has ever experienced.

The Christian contemplative path may be characterized as the *via negativa*: an "apophatic" approach that focuses on a direct encounter with the object of our heart's longing, unmediated by the structures of traditional organized religion. There are three stages to this "way of negation." First, the seeker must surrender to a process of purification, in which all sensual attachments to the sacred are stripped away and all concepts of the nature or even the existence of God are forfeited. This is the period of "purgation" (*via purgativa*).

From that place of spiritual nakedness, the seeker enters into the second phase of her journey, the *via illuminativa*, in which the divine light is poured into the purified vessel of the soul. Because of our habitual ways of seeing, this blinding radiance is at first experienced as darkness. We have to develop new spiritual eyes to absorb the illumination that can only come into a soul emptied of habitual feelings and concepts.

The final stage of the spiritual path is union: *via unitiva*. This occurs when, at least for fleeting moments, the small self merges into the One and disappears. The Christian mystics often use the language of romantic love to describe this melding. It is transformation of the lover (the soul) into the Beloved (God), rendering them inseparable. Every last shred of awareness of the phenomenal world falls away in that mystical absorption.

For John of the Cross, the journey to liberation (union) involves passage through the desert of the unknown. In this process, the seeker suffers the excruciating loss of everything that ever caused her to feel connected to God and assure her that He was with her. Although it may feel like a death, this is the true beginning of the spiritual life.

Teresa of Avila, John's mentor and author of *The Interior Castle*, saw the soul as a beautiful crystal, perfectly clear, circular and womb-like, with many facets leading to the central chamber, from which the Beloved is calling her inward to have union with Him. For Teresa, the path home to God was to simply be still and go within. She calls the contemplative state "the Prayer of Quiet." We can orchestrate our own inner journey only up to a point, Teresa teaches. Then we have to let go, drop into the arms of the unknown, and pray that the Beloved will receive us, replacing all our noisy spiritual efforts with the deep quiet of His loving Presence.

The Hebrew prophets, patriarchs, and matriarchs all had contemplative inclinations. They set aside periods of time for solitude and silence, listening for the voice of the Divine. Moses withdrew from his people for forty nights and ascended Mount Sinai where he encountered the Holy One. Jesus frequently went alone to a quiet place, removing himself from his throng of followers to refill his cup with silence. Mother Mary's response to the sacred mysteries she encountered was to grow quiet, and go within. "Mary treasured all these things, pondering them in her heart" (Luke 2:19). It is said that after the crucifixion, Mary Magdalene set sail for Europe and spent the rest of her life meditating in a cave in France.

The Prophet Muhammad was also contemplative. On the Night of Power, when the Angel Gabriel appeared and commanded him to "recite in the name of the Lord," the Prophet was meditating alone in a cave, as he had done since he was an adolescent. From this divine encounter, Muhammad received instructions for how to worship the One. Following the *Shahada*, the formal declaration of the Oneness of God, *salat* is the second pillar upholding Islam. Five times each day Muslims pause from their activities ɔ remember God. First they engage in ritual ablutions of mouth, hands, and feet, then unfold their prayer rugs and, reciting passages from the Qur'an, prostrate themselves, pressing their foreheads to the floor, in full-body submission to the Divine.

The practice of *dhikr* (remembrance) is essential to Islam. As with devout Jews and Christians, many Muslims strive to engage in "prayer unceasing," keeping the names of God continuously in their minds and hearts. The Qur'an exhorts us: "O you who believe, you shall remember GOD frequently. You shall glorify Him day and night" (33:41–42). This depth of spiritual focus fosters deep inner quiet. It is easy to become distracted by the clamor of the world, but when we cultivate a continuously invitational attitude toward the sacred, we are able, as the Sufis say, to be "in the world, but not of it."

A contemplative approach to life is not just a matter of pursuing a discipline of silent prayer. It is about creating a spaciousness in our days that invites an ongoing encounter with the Divine Presence. This quality of spiritual receptivity requires attention and intention, but it does not have to involve a formal sitting practice.

To live a contemplative life means to consciously put aside the thousand demands of the world and offer ourselves the gift of being in the present moment, alert to the signs of the sacred that are breaking through everywhere, always: watching the sun rising over a still lake; listening—really listening—as your brother reads a Jimmy Santiago Baca poem aloud at a family gathering; stopping everything you're doing when a six-year-old tries to spell the word "love" for the first time; declining yet another invitation to attend a concert, party, or lunch with an acquaintance who would like to get to know you better, and instead taking the evening off to sit on the porch and watch the moon rise. Conversations with loved ones can be contemplative acts. Watering the garden, pulling weeds, slicing vegetables. Writing a real letter on real paper, sending it off with a real stamp.

Sacred Reading

> *During all that time, I never dared to sit down to pray unless I had a book close at hand. My soul was as terrified of praying without a book as it would have been if thrown unarmed onto a raging battlefield. Books were my companions, my consolation, my shield against the explosion of thoughts.*
>
> Teresa of Avila, *The Book of My Life*

I come from a family that bowed at the altar of the written word. Poetry was a temple; poets were the saints and masters. The world's traditional sacred scriptures were admired as jewels of literary genius, rather than upheld as the source of religious truths. Serious fiction was embraced; pop novels tolerated. Our world was the back-to-the-land counterculture of the early 1970s, and it did not include television, so most of what my siblings and I knew about the world beyond our fringe community was from books.

I was aware of almost everything my parents were reading, and I still remember: the poems of T.S. Eliot and Basho, Erica Jong and Gary Snyder; *Be Here Now, Small Is Beautiful, Seth Speaks;* Hermann Hesse, Doris Lessing, Kurt Vonnegut; the *Rubaiyat,* the *Tao Te Ching,* and Kahlil Gibran's *The Prophet.*

What ten-year-old tracks such things? The same light that drew me like a moth to the fire of religion—a flame that did not burn in our house—radiated from the books my parents worshipped. These pages emitted a radiance of their own. I was in awe. The attitude of reverence made it permanently impossible for me to read quickly and superficially. Every encounter with a book became a form of *darshan,* or spiritual transmission, requiring my full attention.

So it is probably not surprising that reading is thoroughly integrated with my spiritual life. I practice and teach a kind of organic version of *lectio divina:* contemplative reading. In Judaism, this method takes the form of Torah study, an essential feature of religious life. In Islam, it involves deep study of the Qur'an and the hadith. Traditionally, *lectio* involves reading short passages from sacred scripture, and then meditating on them, drawing in the essence and allowing it to nourish your soul.

I use an eclectic assortment of readings, involving everything from the classic mystical poetry of the thirteenth-century Persian mystic Rumi and the fifteenth-century Indian poet-saint Mirabai to postmodern masters like Mary Oliver and Antonio Machado. I choose succulent morsels from the Spanish mystics, John of the Cross and Teresa of Avila, as well as contemporary teachers like Pema Chödrön and Ram Dass. Every religion is welcome in my sacred library, and no topic is dismissed as heretical. I find that the language of drugs, sex, and rock and roll can be just as revelatory and holy as the canon of any established religious tradition.

I incorporate this method into my work as a bereavement counselor, where I use a contemplative rather than a cathartic approach. In my retreats I read aloud gems of sacred writing and interweave them with periods of extended silence. People grappling with profound loss can let themselves down into the arms of sacred language, and then rest there. It creates sanctuary. We also write during these sessions, using my friend Natalie Goldberg's "wild mind" approach, in which writing becomes a spiritual practice. This combination of reading, sitting in silence, and sharing our stories has a gentle yet transformational effect. In this way, even our most radical losses and deepest sorrows become opportunities for cultivating a contemplative life.

I am fortunate that my primary vocation—writing—is a built-in contemplative experience. I have to get very quiet inside to access the words that are trying to break through the ground of awareness. I need to remove myself from distraction and become one-pointed. I light a candle and say a simple invocation to begin. I stop often, gaze out the window, watch thunderheads build in the east, spiders spinning egg sacs on my windowsill.

I also try to be true to a regular meditation practice. I start most days with yoga *asanas*, followed by silent sitting, and I close my practice by reading a few pages of whatever book I have picked for my altar. When my children were small, they understood that you do not disturb Mom until this morning ritual is complete and the bedroom door opens. The first note my daughter Jenny ever wrote to me was when she was seven: "Mommy," it said, "Plez wak me up wen yu finsh yur praktx." I knew exactly what she was trying to say.

But it's hard, isn't it? That extra hour of sleep feels so good, and sometimes it is needed. How do we fit in time to sit there "doing nothing" when there is so much of everything demanding our attention? A few years ago when I was in Spain, I visited Teresa of Avila's first convent. I stood in the stone vestibule where visitors have sought counsel from the cloistered Carmelites for five centuries. I rang the bell people would ring during Teresa's time. The voice of the sister on duty resonated clearly through the wooden grill, though I could not even see the outline of her habit.

"How can I help you?" she asked.

"Sister," I said—very formal, very serious—"I would like to write a book about Teresa of Avila that helps American women learn to balance lives of action and contemplation."

The nun chortled. "*Ay, mi hija,*" she said, "as soon as we learn how to do that ourselves, we will be happy to teach you!" And she laughed some more. "You think our

Santa Madre knew how to do that? In her day, there was so much to do all the time she was grateful for a single hour to herself to sit with God. And then, when she finally could be alone, her meditation was often empty and dry. 'Lord!' she would shake her fist at God. 'You fill my heart with longing for you and then you hide yourself from me! Is that any way to treat the ones you love?'"

The sister continued. "These days, by the time we have answered all the monastery emails and baked the cookies we sell at the market, mended our blouses, and sorted the beans, we hardly have a moment left over for prayer." Her voice grew more tender. "Don't be so hard on yourselves, *hija*—that's what I would say. Do the best you can to live simply and love God. I am fairly certain our Mother Teresa would have agreed. Now, is there anything else I can do for you?"

But I couldn't answer. I was weeping.

The Wisdom of the Desert

> *The desert and the dry land will be glad; the wilderness will rejoice and blossom.*
>
> Isaiah 35:1

> *I will lead you into the desert, and there I will speak to your heart.*
>
> Hosea 2:14

Just as fish die if they remain on dry land, so monks remaining away from their cells… lose their determination to persevere in solitary prayer. Therefore, just as fish should go back to the sea, so we must return to our cells, lest remaining outside we forget to watch over ourselves interiorly.

Abbot Anthony, *Desert Father*

A white flower grows in the quietness; let your tongue become that flower.

Mevlana Jalaluddin Rumi

WHEN MY DEAR friends Tessa and Father Dave moved on from their Carmelite community after decades living a monastic life, they did not leave behind the quiet beauty of living simply, with ample solitude and silence. As hermits in the high desert of the Sangre de Cristos, they reached out to an informal circle of friends from around the world who share a dedication to fostering understanding and reconciliation between the Children of Abraham, and formed an online community. In exploring the cultures and spiritualities that grow out of the world's deserts, they are especially interested in the connection between the outer deserts of the Middle East and the American Southwest, and the *inner* desert of contemplative life.

Tessa wrote the foreword to one of my translations of Teresa of Avila, and Father Dave shares my birthday, so we have a special bond. One year Tessa called me just before my birthday.

"We have a present for you."

"Oh goody," I said. "What is it?"

"Two nights alone in the hogan."

The hogan is Tessa's hermitage. It is a one-room Navajo-style octagon made of logs, situated in the middle of a meadow surrounded by piñon, juniper, and scrub oak, on the edge of a mountain creek. Windows in all directions allow Tessa to track the life unfolding around her. Full-moon nights are ecstatically holy for her. She says that the moon wakes her up when it rises and then again just before it sets. Although Tessa has solar electricity, she hides her single reading lamp and all electric cords in a drawer during the day so that there are no signs of technology in sight.

Father Dave lives in a hermitage about a quarter of a mile from Tessa's, and they had agreed that she would sleep on his couch during my visit, so that I could have the hogan to myself. No one else had ever slept in Tessa's hermitage before. This, they both said, was the most valuable thing they could offer me: the gift of deep stillness.

I arrived late in the afternoon the day before my birthday. Tessa and Father Dave had cooked a feast in Father Dave's tiny kitchen, and we stayed up late celebrating our friendship. Then I turned on my flashlight and headed down the forest path. Having grown up in the country, and having visited Tessa at her hermitage the year before, I decided to switch off the light and let my feet find their way in the dark. As John of the Cross sings in his timeless poem *Songs of the Soul* (the precursor to *Dark Night of the Soul*), it is in the darkness that the lover (the soul) slips away from her quiet house for a secret rendezvous in the garden with the Beloved (God).

I rested that night more deeply than I had in months. The next morning, I sat alone on Tessa's porch, a book in my lap and my journal beside me, and spent hours absorbing the spring sunshine, watching jays and wrens chase each other through the willows and cottonwoods bordering the creek and ground squirrels patrol the hogan, waiting for me to go inside so they could sneak up and steal a nibble of Tessa's potted lobelia.

Every once in a while I would read a few pages from Teresa of Avila's *Way of Perfection* or jot down a thought in my notebook, but all I really wanted to do was to sit still and allow the frenetic energy of my daily life to melt like a spoonful of honey in a cup of tea. Later, I took a long walk in the foothills surrounding the hermitage, followed by a nap. By the time I joined Father Dave and Tessa for dinner, I was nearly speechless with childlike joy. Sharing their contemplative life was the most generous present my friends could have given me.

The Desert Fathers and Mothers were a group of fourth-century hermits who withdrew to the wilderness in Egypt, Palestine, Arabia, and Persia to engage in lives of perpetual prayer. They removed themselves from what they perceived as the decadence of the Roman Church to cultivate a direct relationship with the Holy Mystery in the stark desert landscape. The twentieth-century contemplative, Thomas Merton, said of someone following this path, "He had to lose himself in the inner, hidden reality of a self that was transcendent, mysterious, half-known, and lost in Christ."

There was an element of rigorous asceticism to the lives of the Desert Fathers and Mothers. Through solitude, prayer, manual labor, voluntary poverty, fasting, and unmitigated charity toward their neighbors, they strove to cleanse themselves of every desire except the desire for union with God. In this way, the outer desert served as a metaphor for the inner purgation necessary to strip away the false self and find "purity of heart." From this place of apparent emptiness, the desert bursts into bloom and reveals itself as teeming with vitality and wonder.

The key is, as with all mystical traditions, to become free of identification with the individual self. Prolonged periods of silence and solitude loosen the grip of the ego. Saint Anthony remarks, "The prayer of the monk is not perfect until he no longer realizes himself or the fact that he is praying." The Desert Fathers and Mothers were at home in the unknown; they made friends with paradox.

The Desert Mother, Amma Syncletica, describes the extreme asceticism of the hermetic life with feminine pragmatism: "In the beginning there are a great many battles and a good deal of suffering for those who are advancing towards God and afterwards, ineffable joy. It is like those who wish to light a fire; at first they are choked by the smoke and cry, and by this means obtain what they seek...so we must also kindle the divine fire in ourselves through tears and hard work."

Thomas Merton reflects on the relevance of these early Christian masters for the contemporary seeker. "We cannot do exactly what they did," he admits. "But we must be as thorough and as ruthless in our determination to break all spiritual chains, and cast off the domination of alien compulsions, to find our true selves, to discover and develop our inalienable spiritual liberty and use it to build, on earth, the Kingdom of God" (*The Wisdom of the Desert*).

FIRE AND WINE
The Path of Suffering and Exaltation

It is the aim of my pilgrimage on earth to show my brethren by living demonstration how one may serve God with merriment and rejoicing. For he who is full of joy is full of love for men and for all fellow creatures.

Baal Shem Tov

"Where are you going?"
She said, "To that world."
"And where have you come from?"
She answered, "From that world."
"And what are you doing in this world?"
And she said, "I am sorrowing."
"In what way?" they asked of her.
And Rabia replied,
"I am eating the bread of this world,
and doing the work of that world."

Zuleikha, "Rabia Song"

For me, prayer is a surge of the heart; it is a simple look turned
toward Heaven, it is a cry of recognition and of love, embracing
both trial and joy; in a word, something noble, supernatural,
which enlarges my soul and unites it to God. . . . I have not the
courage to look through books for beautiful prayers. . . . I do as
a child who has not learned to read, I just tell our Lord all that I
want and he understands.

Thérèse of Lisieux, *The Story of a Soul*

Overflowing

TWO THINGS ARE guaranteed to hook you up with the God
of Love: sorrowing and rejoicing. You do not need to go
searching for either; they are written into the architecture
of human existence. Youth and beauty ripen and decay.
The man you long for is obsessed with someone else; the
woman you fell in love with has sold her soul to alco-
hol. Someone with whom the fabric of your own life is in-
terwoven dies, and your heart unravels. The foundation
drops out from under you. How can you possibly live in
a world without your loved one in it?

Then, in the midst of unbearable anguish, as you sit in
the sanctuary during the memorial service and the people
around you lift their voices in harmony, singing prayers to
the God of Love, light begins to seep into the torn places
and you are illuminated. Your soul is magnified, infused
with sweetness. The wings of invisible advocates enfold
you and hold you. In spite of your wish to follow your
loved one to the other side, you are welcomed back into

the human family, your rightful place here on Earth made clear, sanctified. At the heart of your deepest loss you discover your forgotten wholeness.

For a moment, death is not the punishment you thought it was. Instead, it is a doorway into the mystery. It is the wind that ruffles the veil between this world and that, affording you glimpses of something greater, something exquisite and vast. Your senses are heightened. Everything becomes almost unbearably beautiful: the rain on the tin roof, a columbine pushing through a crack in the walkway, a slice of buttered toast. Your world has come undone, and you have never felt so alive. You do not dare speak this madness to anyone. They have not yet discovered what you have: that grief is proportionate to love and exponentially enlarges the capacity of our souls, making enough room for it all.

You did not ask for this gift. Who would choose to walk around without skin on her heart, permeable to the suffering of every passing creature? Yet if pressed, you would have to admit that it's worth it. You grieve the torture of a faraway prisoner who momentarily flashes by on your television screen as if he were your own son. And when a magpie lands on the stones of the fountain in your garden and stoops to drink, you can barely contain your rapture.

The God of Love is extravagant, overflowing with riches, lifting and filling the most broken and empty heart, impelling the joyous to share their bounty with the whole world.

Holy Fools

HOLY INTOXICATION IS a universal side effect of the direct encounter with the God of Love. Sacred poems of Judaism, Christianity, and Islam share the metaphor of wine and spiritual drunkenness. "Let him kiss me with the kisses of his mouth," cries the Bride in the Song of Songs, "for thy love is better than wine." When Jesus commenced his ministry, following forty days and nights of fasting in the wilderness, his first act was to turn water into wine. Rumi continuously compares the Holy One to the Cupbearer and His love to wine, which delivers the soul beyond all reason to a realm of pure love.

Another metaphor common to the three Abrahamic faiths is the image of fire. The flames of love consume the soul who has caught a glimpse of the Divine, and reduce her to the purest spiritual substance. An angel of the Lord appeared to Moses at the heart of a bush that burned but was not consumed and revealed the identity of the One God. After the crucifixion of Christ, as the disciples grieved in an upper room in Jerusalem, tongues of flame appeared and touched each of them, clarifying and transforming their hearts, minds, and speech. Sufi poetry continually invokes the fire of longing for union with the Beloved, a burning for which the seeker ardently prays. In each tradition, the soul is the moth who rushes into the flame that will annihilate her.

The Garden is another unifying image in Abrahamic wisdom writings. King Solomon and John of the Cross refer to the secret rendezvous of lover and Beloved in the garden of the heart. Rumi compares intimacy with Allah to the fragrance of a rose garden, which is all the soul wants. The garden serves as the place of refuge, where we can cool off from the raging fire of yearning and sober up from the inebriating effects of the divine encounter. It represents consolation and delight—Paradise.

All three of these metaphors imply an absence of pietism and lack of self-control. In spite of the universal passion expressed through such archetypes, many of us harbor the illusion that spiritual masters are different from us, the primary distinction being that we are caught by our emotions while they hover above the human predicament in a realm of serene graciousness. We endow our sages with the virtue of unflappability, and are quick to remove them from their pedestals when they exhibit desire or disappointment.

The greatest saints and mystics were plagued by all the same challenges the rest of us grapple with—often more so. There is plenty of reason to imagine that if Joan of Arc or the poet Hafez had been born into contemporary Western society, they would be medicated for psychosis rather than exalted as spiritual masters. The line between genius and madness has always been a fluid one. Radical gifts seem to be accompanied by equally potent imbalances. Many brilliant artists, poets, and spiritual leaders suffer from depression and substance abuse.

Letters preserved from Hildegard of Bingen and Teresa of Avila indicate that they both obsessed on the affections of the people they loved; they were petulant and demanding when they didn't get the attention they wanted. Francis of Assisi once scrambled to the top of a new monastery under construction, tore the tiles from the roof, and threw them to the ground, declaring that they were too expensive and violated his cherished ideal of voluntary simplicity. Furious with the Israelites for resorting to worship of the Golden Calf in his absence, Moses smashed the first set of tablets he received on Mount Sinai and had to go back up the mountain for another forty days to collect a new set.

Every tradition has its holy fools, and entire religious orders have been created from their seemingly irreverent behavior. The legendary Baal Shem Tov (Master of the Good Name), founder of Chasidic Judaism, defied the stuffy religiosity of his day and danced in the streets with the Torah scroll as if it were his lover—which it was—and multitudes of Jews have followed in his ecstatic footsteps for over two centuries. It has been said that the Catholic Church did not know what to do with its mystics—whose tendency to communicate directly and fervently with the Divine circumvented accepted institutional channels—and so canonized them as saints, instead of condemning them as heretics. The whirling dervishes established their primary practice to emulate their master, Mevlana Jalaluddin Rumi, who, devastated by the loss of his closest spiritual companion, Shams of Tabriz, began turning one day in the middle of the busy marketplace and entered a state of profound ecstasy, from which he never recovered.

Mystics dwell in the zone between unbearable suffering and transcendent joy. Heirs to the human condition, which administers pain and delight in unpredictable doses, we all have the opportunity to let our experiences break us open to a place beyond the dualities of good and evil, right and wrong, self and the Divine. From this perspective, the question about how God could possibly allow the deaths of children in wars and the clear-cutting of old growth redwood forests loses its teeth, at least for fleeting moments. Then we drop back down into the flames of our pain, where our wounds are cauterized and we are brought back into the quiet joy of the most ordinary moments: snow drifting on the window ledge while we sit warm and safe inside.

Singing the Divine Names

SUFFERING IS NOT always the mark of an awakened consciousness, of course, and ecstasy does not always signal proximity to the Holy One. My own inner life used to be characterized by soaring highs and devastating lows. As I grow older, the spiritual path becomes less personal. Sometimes I lose the experiencer altogether for a while and there is just the experience, whether one of emptiness or plenitude. There are days when, after hours of writing about the God of Love, I set out on the trail through the foothills behind my house and find myself floating in a sublime state. I am fully content then, quiet as a stone inside.

Maybe this is what John of the Cross means when he speaks about the soul who starts off suckling from the breasts of the Divine. Eventually, God sees that we have matured enough to take our own seat and chew our own food. Weaning feels like banishment. Yet, from time to time, we are still given those moments of sweetness when the divine elixir comes pouring through that secret hole in the roof of our soul-mouth and we are directly nourished. The desert we have been learning to navigate bursts into bloom.

At those times, every terrible thing that has ever happened to me makes perfect sense. When I am in that transcendental state, everything falls into place and finds its perfection in the Big Cosmic Picture that unfolds across the horizons of my consciousness. This even happens when I am overwhelmed by loss. Sometimes especially then.

Maybe it's brain chemistry. Maybe it's denial, illusion, dissociation. I don't care. It feels like grace. I do not cling to it, but I appreciate it. I know how fleeting these glimpses of perfection are. Soon enough I will again perceive just how complicated and unfortunate it all is. Once I've returned to my senses, I cannot even imagine seeing anything beautiful and perfect about death, divorce, and sexual abuse. Loss is just loss again. Injustice is intolerable.

Yet haven't devotional practices always been associated with heightened states of awareness? Weren't they designed for that? If we did not have moments of ecstasy, what would motivate us to show up for the hard work that characterizes the bulk of the inner life? If we did not periodically lose ourselves in spiritual drunkenness, we might be tempted to take it all too seriously—dogma and fanaticism, institutional politics, ourselves—and forget that the Holy One does not live in the boxes human beings so elaborately construct to contain her. During moments of exaltation, the God of Love breaks the levees and floods our hearts, drowning all obstacles.

Every spiritual tradition has its own version of chanting the Divine Names. Research in brain science has revealed that the repetition of certain sounds sends electrical signals that balance neurotransmitters and stimulate a state of heightened awareness and peace. The ancient languages of Hebrew, Arabic, and Sanskrit seem best suited to effect these neurological shifts. Rabbi Shefa Gold describes the power of devotional chanting as "part science, part ecstasy, and part mystery."

I am rarely happier than when I am singing to the Sacred. The joy intensifies when I am surrounded by other voices singing with me. I am a longtime practitioner of Hindu *kirtan* (devotional chanting). *Kirtan* uses a call and response structure, where the person leading the chant sings a mantra (sacred phrase) and the rest of the group responds. The words and the melody are simple. Accompanied by traditional Indian drone instruments, bells, and hand drums, the energy of the chant gradually rises until it reaches a crescendo of devotional outpouring. Some contemporary *kirtan wallahs* (chant leaders) have begun to incorporate nontraditional instruments, such as guitars, into the mix. Although *kirtan* is a Hindu ritual, it inevitably carries me beyond the particulars of language and culture to a place of vibrant connectedness to the Nameless One.

I also experience the transformational power of sacred sound while chanting the ancient Jewish prayers such as the *kaddish* (the traditional mourner's prayer), which extols the boundless mystery of the Divine, the *Shema*: "Hear, O Israel, God is One," and the heart-rending melodies of Yom Kippur. I taste it when I sing the Jesus prayer in Greek, *Kyrie Eleison, Christe Eleison*: "Lord have mercy, Christ have mercy." As I sit with Sufis and affirm the oneness of Allah in song, we are rowing the boat of prayer, and I feel myself gliding into the numinous. When vocal prayer is combined with movement—lifting the arms and bowing to the left and the right in *zikr*, turning in slow circles during Sufi dancing, bending the knees and swaying in place while *davening* at the synagogue, bowing at the altar and genuflecting in church—the practice takes on an even more penetrating quality.

Listening to sacred music can be almost as potent for me as making it. Native American drumming and Tibetan toning, African American gospel music, the Catholic Mass and Shaker hymns, all contain a secret combination that unlocks my heart and leads me into the chamber of God-consciousness. When the music ends, the silence that pours into the empty space left by the song reverberates through every cell of my body, aligning my breath with my spirit and my aspirations with my disappointments, and a weariness at the core of my soul drains away.

Whether I am leading or participating, singing or listening, music is a magic carpet that almost never fails to lift me. American chant master Krishna Das makes it clear that he does not engage in this practice to be good and score spiritual points. "I sing to save my life," he says. Sacred song is an in-breath of holy longing, an out-breath of devotion. Singing to the God of Love builds a temple, a mosque, a kingdom here on Earth.

In Praise of the Ordinary

THE MOST RADIANT exemplars of each faith tradition seem to share this common theme: they perceived the extraordinary in the ordinary and celebrated it. The Baal Shem Tov taught that we should dedicate the whole of our lives to serving God with joy. Nothing, he said, is separate from the Holy One. Nature is imbued with the Divine, and creation is an ongoing process, unfolding before our eyes, as well as within us. "The world is new to us every morning," the Baal Shem Tov said. "This is God's gift; and every man should believe he is reborn each day."

For the Baal Shem Tov, prayer was not a matter of petitioning the Holy One for favors, but rather a wholehearted offering of the individual self to the eternal being of God, for the purpose of becoming one with Him. "Our heart is the altar," he said. "In whatever you do let a spark of the holy fire burn within you, so that you may fan it into a flame." The flaming of the heart creates a state of living bliss, which radiates into every arena of life.

The Baal Shem Tov challenged the rigidity of Talmudic law and dispensed with asceticism. He celebrated the body as holy and considered physical delight to be a manifestation of the glory of God. Like many great religious figures in history, he broke existing taboos and extended himself to people considered to be outcasts and sinners. Since God is all that is, the Baal Shem Tov taught, evil is a misconception, set right by expanding our consciousness to include all things as manifestations of the Divine. He endeavored to treat all beings with mercy and righteousness, and so to call out of them their own merciful, righteous natures.

Although the Baal Shem Tov was a radical reformer in his time, contemporary Hasidism has in many respects become more conservative than Orthodox Judaism. Nevertheless, the ecstatic legacy of "the Master of the Good Name" pervades the heart of Judaism. The portal to the Transcendent opens through the Immanent. Song and dance, food and family, nature and each other are all manifestations of the Sacred, worthy of unending praise.

The French mystic Thérèse of Lisieux (not to be confused with Teresa of Avila), is affectionately known as "the Little Flower," and she referred to her own spiritual path as "the Little Way." Although she is revered for her humility and simplicity, all her life Thérèse was determined to become a saint. By the time she died in 1897 at the age of twenty-four, she had achieved her childhood ambition. Yet it was in forgetting herself, rather than being elevated to some rarefied spiritual status, that Thérèse's sanctity shone.

A true mark of her illumination, Thérèse placed no more significance on her mistakes than she did on her triumphs. The important thing was to melt into the heart of the Divine. "If through weakness I should chance to fall," Thérèse wrote, "may a glance from Your Eyes straightway cleanse my soul, and consume all my imperfections—as fire transforms all things into itself." She suffered criticism and accepted praise with equal quietude, redirecting discomfort and delight as offerings to "merciful love."

Like many saints before her, Thérèse prayed to participate in the suffering of Jesus. As with Francis of Assisi, who bore the marks of the crucifixion on his own body, Thérèse embraced the onset of tuberculosis as an opportunity for kinship with her Lord. On the night before Good Friday, as she lay down to sleep, Thérèse reports, "I felt something like a bubbling stream mounting to my lips." The next morning, she coughed up blood, and her suspicions were confirmed. In Thérèse's day, tuberculosis was a death sentence, and that meant she would not only share in Christ's agony but soon would be joining him in a place beyond all suffering. While her illness did involve a harrowing physical ordeal, Thérèse also suffered a "dark night of the soul," in which she wrestled with the most core elements of her faith, continually giving her internal turmoil back to God.

Thérèse of Lisieux's autobiography, *The Story of a Soul*, published after her death, sparked the imaginations of millions, and elevated a young woman who believed she was invisible to the status of a spiritual superstar. As with Francis, Thérèse's popularity extends far beyond the borders of the Roman Catholic Church. Her emphasis on finding and adoring the Holy in everyday life has broad appeal to people of all faiths. In dedicating our smallest actions to the God of Love, Thérèse believed that we are contributing to the transformation of the whole world.

Maura "Soshin" O'Halloran is a twentieth-century mirror to the soul of Thérèse of Lisieux. An Irish Catholic who is venerated as a Buddhist saint, Maura also died young—at age twenty-seven—by which time she too had accomplished a spiritual goal that most people never achieve in a long life of religious effort. Halfway through a year of rigorous Zen training at a remote monastery in Japan, Maura experienced *satori*, a spontaneous awakening in which all things found their rightful place in a unified field of consciousness, and she was filled with ecstasy, quickly followed by an unbroken wave of compassion for all beings.

For Maura, this experience was a kind of death. There was nothing left to strive for. The only thing that made any sense was to dedicate herself to being of service. Not long after her awakening, Maura decided to leave the monastery, where she was being groomed as the first woman teacher in her lineage, and return home to Ireland in hopes of giving herself to the task of alleviating suffering in the larger world. On her way through Thailand the bus that was carrying her crashed, and Maura O'Halloran was killed. A Zen master who never denied her Christian roots, Maura is an ongoing example of abundant charity distilled into a singular, short, illuminated life.

Rabia Al-Adawiyya was a Sufi ecstatic who lived in eighth-century Iraq. Most of what we know about Rabia comes from the stories told about her and the spontaneous love poems to God that she spoke aloud, as Rumi did, and which her followers wrote down. But the most enduring gift of Rabia's legacy is her absolute insistence on loving God for God alone, rather than a means of bargaining with the Divine for spiritual rewards. "O God!" she prayed. "If I worship You for fear of Hell, burn me in Hell, and if I worship You in hope of Paradise, exclude me from Paradise. But if I worship You for Your Own sake, begrudge me not Your everlasting Beauty."

Rabia was born into a poor family during a time of extended drought. When her father died, Rabia joined a caravan traveling through the desert. A band of robbers attacked the group, kidnapped Rabia, and sold her to slave traders. Rabia's new master demanded that she engage in hard labor from dawn to dusk. The worst part of this arrangement was that it interfered with the young mystic's longing to be with God, so she regularly spent all night in prayer. She intensified her practice by fasting.

One night, Rabia's owner awoke to the sound of singing. He followed the music to the roof, where he found the slave girl lost in ecstatic praise of Allah. A radiance emanated from her head and lit up the entire house. Quietly, he returned to bed and pondered what he had witnessed. In the morning, the master called Rabia to him and acknowledged her as a great saint. He offered to free her and asked her to remain in his household so that he could serve her. Rabia asked that he allow her instead to enter the desert where she could live as a hermit in continual remembrance of God. The man granted her request.

Rabia spent the remainder of her life in passionate devotion to the God of Love. In spite of her wish to live in solitude, many disciples gathered around her. Rabia's outer life was simple. Her only possessions were a chipped jug, a mat made of woven rushes, and the brick she used as a pillow. But the basket of her inner life spilled over with bounty.

"Oh God," Rabia exclaimed, "Whenever I listen to the voice of anything you have made—the rustling of the trees, the trickling of the water, the cries of birds, the flickering of shadow, the roar of the wind, the song of the thunder, I hear it saying: God is One! Nothing can be compared with God!"

I can't help but notice that many of companions I have gathered around me in my own life are Fools of God. They burn with an inner fire that consumes them, causing no end of turmoil, yet compensating them with seductive bursts of exaltation. Whether or not they believe in a personified deity called God, these are beings for whom the sacred permeates every element of their lives, overflowing in creative self-expression.

Jenny Bird composes song after song to the God of Love disguised as a beautiful man, as a pair of sleeping children, as the way friends hold each other up in times of despair. Justine paints her way to the Nameless Sacred across the landscape of ceramic tile. "Making art is really just my way of living, aloud," she says. "What I really want is to be more alive while making art—and also while making salad or making love." Bill perceives the *Shekhinah* in the clouds that gather over Taos Mountain on summer mornings and in the faces of his congregation who kneel at the altar and sing the hymns of their Spanish ancestors. He translates this indwelling presence into the icons he paints of classic Christian figures imbued with a universal light. My brother carries on the legacy of our father, hearing the anguished cry for freedom in the works of the great poets of every age, echoing inside his own thirsty soul.

Each of these artists suffers for his art. All of them achieve exalted states in the process of creating. They endure the common wound of yearning, dissatisfaction, and self-imposed isolation. They also have a shared tendency to gasp in childlike wonder in response to the way sunlight falls across an expanse of winter grasses, weep at a new rendition of Leonard Cohen's "Hallelujah," leap with childlike delight when they receive an email from a loved one trekking in Nepal or visiting New York City. Like me, they feel everything deeply and would not trade this heightened sensitivity for anything. The God of Love peeks from behind the curtain of these holy moments,

beckoning us into the heart of the human condition, revealing our legacy as seekers of the True, as lovers of the
Beautiful, as servants of All That Is.

AFTERWORD
Walking the Interspiritual Path

A LITTLE MORE than a hundred years ago, Swami Vivekananda—beloved disciple of the God-intoxicated Indian saint Sri Ramakrishna—came to the West and dazzled the first World's Parliament of Religions in Chicago with his vision of the essential interconnectedness of all spiritual paths. The event marked the birth of a global dialog of faiths, a conversation that continues even today. The interfaith movement has been characterized by the sincere effort on the part of religious believers from all the world's major faith traditions to build tolerance, trust, and mutual understanding. In light of the historical atrocities committed by powerful institutions in the name of God, such dialog has been both liberating and healing.

Now, at the dawn of a new century, it's time to go deeper. It's not enough to seek an intellectual orientation toward other traditions. We need to plunge into their mystic heart and let them transform us.

This is exactly what Ramakrishna was up to. He did not politely approach Christianity and agree to tolerate it. He enfolded Christ into his own blazing heart and met him there, in the fire of love. He kept a picture of the child Jesus and Mother Mary on his altar—along with Kali, Krishna, Tara, and the Buddha—and offered incense to them every morning. He repeated the name of Allah throughout the day with profound devotion and experienced a vision in which the Prophet Muhammad merged into his own body. He adored the Divine Mother in every form; it was through her that he experienced all differences reconciled. Ramakrishna actively practiced diverse faith traditions, and their particular objects of devotion regularly brought him to tears of ecstasy.

Immersion in the well of any single spiritual tradition seems to dissolve the forms that limit the Divine. Repetition of any of the Holy Names carries us to a place that transcends all naming, where we rest in the One Reality. Ramakrishna says that it is not necessary to renounce the formalities of religion. When you place your devotion at the feet of whatever spiritual ideal is most natural to you, "formalities of every kind will simply disappear from your being."

I'd like to offer a few suggestions for activating your interspiritual quest.

Choose at least one religious tradition different from your own and participate in a service. If you are a Jew, consider taking communion at a Christian church that permits you to receive the Eucharist, and taste the Unknowable on your tongue. If you are a Buddhist, attend a Torah study group and engage in deep inquiry. If you are an agnostic, join in the Dances of Universal Peace and let your heart fly open. Don't be just an observer. Participate. Suspend your disbelief and show up as fully as you can.

Make an extra effort to explore the beauty of Islam. During a time when the political dialog and media messages have demonized Islam and labeled all Muslims as Arabs and all Arabs as terrorists, it is especially important to vanquish the cartoon images we may have in our minds about our Muslim brothers and sisters. Recall that for seven centuries, during the Convivencia in Spain, Jews, Christians, and Muslims not only lived side by side in an atmosphere of religious tolerance, but they also actively collaborated on some of the most important works of art, architecture, literature, mathematics, science, and mystical teachings in the history of Western culture. This all happened under Muslim rule. The commitment to welcoming people of all faiths is still a beacon that shines from the heart of Islam.

It's natural to feel shy when you enter the sacred spaces of other religions. But you may be surprised by how delighted people are that you would show interest in and respect for what is dear to them. Don't be afraid that they are going to try to convert you if you step into their midst. Disarm your heart and let yourself feel the love your hosts have for their Beloved. You may never return to that particular church or synagogue, mosque or zendo. You don't need to. But when we say yes to the God of Love in an unfamiliar, and potentially uncomfortable form, locks fly off the doors of the heart, making more room for the Mystery to dwell there.

If the impact of one of these encounters is especially profound, you may want to see if you can deepen the relationship. Find a teacher who can guide you into the heart of another faith tradition while respecting your commitment to an interspiritual life. Study the holy texts of that tradition. Familiarize yourself with the liturgical cycles and observe the festivals. Look for the unifying teachings, rather than the dogmas that separate us.

Invent your own prayers. It is not necessary to relegate this sacred function to religious professionals. You have every right to compose sacred language. I remember the first time I dared to speak to the Divine in front of the world. My friend Father Bill asked me to write a prayer in honor of Saint Teresa of Avila, whose works I had translated, and offer it to his congregation on her feast day. I, a Jew, offer a prayer before Catholics in their own church? Empowered by his belief in me, yet simultaneously remembering that it was not about me, I dipped into my heart and discovered that the prayer that emerged was the Holy One calling out to the Holy One.

When a significant life event occurs—a death, a birth, a wedding, a divorce—create your own ritual to honor it. Have a Jewish-Hindu-Sufi wedding and write your own vows. Chant the *Tibetan Book of the Dead* in the ear of your grandfather as he lies dying, read him his favorite psalms, invite everyone in the room to sit in silence with him as he draws his final breaths. Bless your new baby with sage from the Southwestern desert, holy water from Assisi, the poetry of Rumi and Basho and Dickinson. Attend a birth and welcome the infant to this world with a song.

When our daughter died so suddenly, we cast about for a ritual to contain the wildness of our loss. No single tradition provided what we were searching for, so we instinctively cobbled together what we needed from various sources. Seven women prepared her body according to Jewish custom and read prayers from all faiths while they were working. Another friend stayed up all night building a casket of red cedar, shaped like a cradle. We brought her body home for a twenty-four-hour vigil, so that her friends and family could say good-bye. Each of her loved ones brought a note or a special object to be burned with her body. A Catholic priest and a Buddhist nun blessed her. We chanted all night in Sanskrit, English, and Arabic. For the seven days following her death, a *minyan* gathered to say the Mourner's Kaddish at sunset. In the tradition of my Jewish ancestors, we unveiled her tombstone on the one-year anniversary, and included Native American prayers and drumming. This tapestry of spiritual resources wove a net that held me when the world that I knew crumbled from under me.

Be the prophet that you are. Reclaim your true voice, which is the Divine voice. Did you love to draw and paint as a child? Buy yourself a special container and fill it with art supplies. Then, instead of watching television to zone out after work, put on some music, spread out sheets of paper, a cup of water for your brushes, a pile of magic markers or colored pencils, and play.

Sing! Did someone once tell you that your voice wasn't good enough? They were wrong. Join a singing group and remember that long-ago thrill of lifting your voice in unison or harmony with a circle of other voices. For as long as there have been humans, they have been singing. "Make a joyful noise unto the Lord, all the earth: make a loud noise, and rejoice, and sing praise" (Psalm 98:4–5). When we are singing to the God of Love, the God of Love is singing to the world.

Reach out to the Divine Feminine. On a piece of paper, write down the one thing you most wish to give up, the issue or emotion that you feel poses the biggest obstacle to your awakening. Is it envy, bitchiness, low self-esteem? In traditional cultures, the Sacred Mother is the one dedicated to winning her children's liberation at any cost. Trust in that. When you have written down your hindrance, take the piece of paper outside, place it in a pit in the ground or hold it over a bowl, and light it on fire. Ask the Mother to take this thing from you. Mean it. Because (wisdom has it) if you do not, she may come take it from you anyway, whether or not you are ready to let go.

Rest. You do not need to be Jewish to practice some version of Shabbat, nor do you have to designate an entire day each week as a Sabbath. Simply make a commitment to regularly disengage from the ordinary compulsions that drive your life. Set aside a period of time to cease from mindless doing and engage in conscious being. Let this act be a gift to yourself and an offering to the God of Love.

Don't believe everything you think. When your mind starts to stack up its stories to prove to you that you have been wronged or you have been wrong, that nobody loves you or that everybody wants something from you, take a deep breath. Remind yourself that just because you think something doesn't make it true. I have been amazed again and again by the power of this simple mindfulness practice. When I start to feel myself spinning into anxiety, I try to suggest to myself the possibility that what I believe to be the case probably isn't. The knots inside me loosen, and I can begin to be with things as they really are.

Mindfulness practice is harder to do with powerful emotions and traumatic circumstances. When an intimate relationship is ending and you find out that your partner is being intimate with someone else, the sword of jealousy can shred your most spiritual ideals to ribbons. When a loved one dies, the foundation of your world shatters and there is no ground to ground your practice. The mere suggestion that you breathe through your grief and try to be present with it is enough to make you want to break something. I know.

So don't do anything fancy. Just rest in your groundlessness and witness what happens. Be willing to not know. See if the God of Love shows up when you fire all the other gods. The god of "I'm a good person; bad things shouldn't happen to me." The "only-people-who-look-like-I-do-are-worthy" god. The god who makes sense.

The gods you put in boxes bar your way to the Infinite. Let them go.

Learning to surrender to your pain is a great way to grow a robust soul and a compassionate heart. But we also need joy. Make time for activities that uplift you. Try this version of Natalie Goldberg's "writing practice." Get together with a small group of friends, read a poem you love out loud, choose a line as a writing prompt, dismiss the editor that reigns inside your head, and spend half an hour writing as fast as you can from your heart. Then read what you wrote to the group. Don't give any disclaimers ahead of time or apologize afterwards.

After each member has read, thank the person, pause for a moment, and go on to the next one, without commentary. I have rarely felt more supported than I have felt in writing groups where we maintained this holy silence after reading; few sacred practices have ever catapulted me into more ecstatic states. You can organize a gathering like this wherever you are, with as many or as few members as you like.

I am aware that what works for me may not fit with your world. When I was exposed to all those different faith traditions in my youth, they were presented with equal value, so I never believed otherwise. I'm like a child who grows up with two gay parents, for whom homosexuality is as natural as hair color. It is not a stretch for me to attend Catholic Mass and sing hymns to Jesus one day and participate in a silent Buddhist meditation retreat the next. But you may be grappling with a lifelong message

that tells you that all Muslims are terrorists, or that anyone who does not accept Jesus Christ as their personal
Lord and Savior is going to hell. I honor your challenge
and commend you for being willing to reach beyond the
boundaries of what you know.

Do not abdicate your power, or your responsibility
to repair this broken world. Old images of holiness are
beginning to fall away. We are realizing that true contemplatives do not always gaze serenely from behind a veil
of detachment. Seasoned spiritual practitioners are just
as likely as anyone else to burst into tears when someone hurts their feelings and bounce out of their chairs like
happy children when they are invited to go to the mov-
ies. A distinguishing mark of the adept on the path is that
the protective covering around the ego has slipped or
been stripped away, and an unmistakable simplicity and
spontaneity infuses her interactions. She will wail against
injustice, delight in praising the Divine, and rest in profound contemplation of the Mystery. She is unpredictable,
authentic, and exactly like you.

While there is much to be learned from teachers—
both past and present—the time of the awakened guru
is giving way to a collective awakening. But we are
not letting go lightly. We have been conditioned to set
our sages apart and project our salvation onto them.
We lose patience with ourselves for not being enough;
we condemn ourselves for being too much. We forget
that the path to God is bound up with our life in the
world. Evidence of our spiritual mastery lies in our

ever-deepening, continuously expanding humanity. The trick is to be as fully present as possible to the holiness of each moment. We are challenged to embrace, yet not identify with, all that is. This requires practice: meditation practice, relationship practice, social action practice. It is built on nobodyness training and yet is dependent on somebodyness experience.

Waking up is a community affair. Jewish wisdom suggests that the Messiah will not be an extrasmart, radiantly beautiful, superpowerful human being who will descend from on high to resolve our differences and repair the damage we have inflicted on one another and on the planet we share. Rather, we are beginning to suspect that redemption is up to all of us. We each need to bring the best of who we are to the spiritual table and offer our own imperfect selves as the medicine for the critically ill spirit of humanity. This includes our despair and our ecstatic insights, the shadow we are most ashamed of and the crazy wisdom with which we astonish even ourselves. Equipped with exactly what we already are, and drawing from the ancient wisdom traditions available to us, we come together to set all beings free.

In a fit of iconoclasm, many of us have been tempted to toss out the traditions of organized religion as we try to make our own way home to Spirit. Many gifts have emerged from this revolution: liberation from patriarchal dominance, increased awareness of the importance of psychological health along the path of awakening, and an abiding regard for indigenous wisdom ways. But we have also found ourselves spiritually bankrupt in some crucial spheres. The world's religious traditions have collected a series of vital tools to help us build a life that includes heightened consciousness of the sacred and a shared sense of accountability to all beings, and we would be foolish to reject them out of hand.

In spite of the undeniable history of abuses committed in the name of religion, the monotheistic faiths offer innumerable points of access to the realm of love. We would do well to revisit the teachings and practices so carefully engineered over millennia to invoke the God of Love and bring Him into our midst. By saying yes to the best of our own heritage and entering the holiest grounds of one another's faith traditions, we may be able to usher in an age of love within our own lifetime. We can only do this together. Through a process of perpetual discernment and "prayer unceasing" we may dive into the well of each faith and emerge with the treasure that connects us all.

GRATITUDE

I AM GRATEFUL to a vast tribe of beings who made this book come true, especially those teachers who illumined a path of interspiritual love for me to follow home to the heart: Neem Karoli Baba, Murshid Samuel Lewis, Hazrat Inayat Khan and Pir Valayat Inayat Khan, Reb Zalman Schacter-Shalomi, and Father Thomas Keating. Thank you, Ram Dass, my lifelong teacher and elder guru-brother, whose voice is so integrated with my own that I cannot even tell the difference: you brought me to this feast. I am also grateful to all my UNM-Taos students over the past two decades who enthusiastically embrace the oneness at the heart of all the world's religious traditions.

Special thanks to my family who has always supported my obsession with all things spiritual, especially my sister, Amy Starr, my ongoing source of fun when it all gets a little too serious. Thanks to my soul-sister, Jenny Bird, for reading every word I write and blessing it. Thank you to my husband, Ganga Das (Jeff Little), who lives these teachings and doesn't have to talk about it. He also listened to every chapter during those magical hours when we sat on our porch with a glass of wine at sunset.

Thank you to my mentors, Charlene McDermott and Asha Greer. Thank you to two women who have been the shining Shams to my inner Rumi: Gabrielle Herbertson and Azima Melita Kolin. Thank you, Elaine Sutton, for naming this book. Tender gratitude to my spiritual siblings, Father Bill McNichols, Tessa Bielecki, and Father Dave Denny. Thanks to Marie Rubie for modeling the pure heart of a child of God. Thanks to Tania Casselle and Sara Morgan for assistance with research and ongoing encouragement. I honor the living prophets I have met who have dedicated the whole of their lives to bearing witness to the God of Love through courageous acts of social justice: Father John Dear, Father Daniel Berrigan, Elizabeth McAlister, Susan Crane, Rose Marie Berger, and Robert Ellsberg. Thank you, Tim Farrington, for teaching me how to sit in the fire and allow it to do its transformational work. Thank you, Bob Thompson, for your wisdom, humor, and unconditional support. Thanks to Andrew Harvey who encouraged me to unleash my wild heart. Thank you, Krishna Das, for pressing the names of God into so many hearts. I am grateful to those who have given themselves to the task of communicating divine oneness through gatherings and film: Will Keepin and Cynthia Brix, and Kell Kearns and Cynthia Lukas.

To all who read early versions of the manuscript and provided invaluable feedback, my deep gratitude: Jonathan Sobol, Latifa Weinman, Hamza Weinman, Andy

Gold, Rameshwar Das, Rabbi David Stein, Jean Jacques Danon, and Netanel Miles-Yepes.

Finally, my profound gratitude to my Monkfish publisher, Paul Cohen, who encouraged me to dispense with objectivity and write from the heart. His faith in me made this process a truly ecstatic journey. And to Toinette Lippe, who came out of retirement to edit this book: I am grateful. It has been an honor to work so closely with someone who changed the face of publishing in America and introduced us to a cast of teachers and teachings whose contribution to the compendium of contemporary spiritual literature is inestimable. Toinette's brilliant insights, high standards, and exquisite tenderness guided me. I do not know how to begin to repay all that you have given me, so I bow to you here, with love.

NOTES

Introduction

"Odes Of Solomon," in *The Odes and Psalms of Solomon*, edited by Rendel Harris and Alphonse Mingana (London: Longmans, Green, 1920), as quoted in *The Enlightened Heart: An Anthology of Sacred Poetry*, edited by Stephen Mitchell (New York: HarperCollins, 1989).

Ibn 'Arabi, "O Marvel," from *Tarjuman al-Ashwaq*, in *The Mystics of Islam*, translated by Reynold A. Nicholson (London: J. Bell, 1914).

Mevlana Jalaluddin Rumi, "I Profess the Religion of Love."

Wayne Teasdale, *The Mystic Heart: Discovering a Universal Spirituality in the World's Religions* (Novato, CA: New World Library, 1999).

Murshid Samuel Lewis, *The Jerusalem Trilogy: Song of the Prophets* (Novato, CA: Prophecy Pressworks, 1975).

Toward the One

Andrew Harvey, Gospel of Thomas, Logion 77, in *The Essential Mystics: The Soul's Journey into Truth* (Minneapolis, MN: Book Sales, 1998).

All Creation Praises God

Psalm 93, in *Shma: A Concise Weekly Siddur*, translated
by Rabbi Zalman Schachter-Shalomi (Boulder, CO:
Albion-Andalus, 2010).

Hazrat Inayat Khan, "There Is Only One Holy Book," in
The Gayan (N.p.: Omega, 1983, 1988, 2005).

Reluctant Prophets

Amos 3:1–7, in *The Hebrew Prophets*, translated by Rabbi
Rami Shapiro (Woodstock, VT: Skylight Paths, 2004).

Karen Armstrong, *The 4,000-Year Quest of Judaism,
Christianity and Islam* (New York: Ballantine, 1993).

Longing for the Beloved

Song of Songs, in *Song of Songs: A New Translation*, translated by Ariel Bloch and Chana Bloch (Berkeley:
University of California Press, 1995).

Mevlana Jalaluddin Rumi, "I've Had Enough," in
Rumi: Hidden Music, translated by Melita Kolin and
Maryam Mafi (London: Thorsons, 2001).

Radical Wonderment

Mevlana Jalaluddin Rumi, "One Morning a Beloved
Said to Her Lover," in William Chittick, *The Sufi Path
of Love: The Spiritual Teachings of Rumi* (Albany, NY:
SUNY Press, 1983).

"But if I Am to Perceive God," Meister Eckhart.

James Farris, "Thinking about God," unpublished
PowerPoint presentation.

Etty Hillesum, *An Interrupted Life: Letters from Westerbork*
(New York: Henry Holt, 1996).

Welcoming the Stranger

Mevlana Jalaluddin Rumi, "The Guesthouse," in The
Essential Rumi, translated by Coleman Barks (San
Francisco, CA: HarperSanFrancisco, 1996).

Robert V. Thompson, *A Voluptuous God: A Christian Heretic
Speaks* (Incline Village, NV: CopperHouse, 2007).

Sacred Service

Abraham Joshua Heschel, *God in Search of Man: A
Philosophy of Judaism* (New York: Farrar, Straus and
Giroux, 1976).

Tessa Bielecki, *Holy Daring: An Outrageous Gift to Modern
Spirituality from Saint Teresa, the Grand Wild Woman of
Avila* (Rockport, MA: Element, 1994).

Mercy

"Return Again," music by Schlomo Carlebach, lyrics
by Rafael-Simkba Kahn. © Schlomo Carlebach. All
rights reserved.

William Treacy and Raphael Levine, *He Is My Brother:
The Bonding of a Priest and Rabbi over 25 Years* (N.p.:
Peanut Butter Publishing, 2007).

"Saint Josephine Bakhita," *Saints.SQPN.com*, http://
saints.sqpn.com/saint-josephine-bakhita.

Indwelling Presence

Bernard of Clairvaux, "Mary, Star of the Sea."

All quotations from Dame Julian of Norwich are the
author's own translation.

Abraham Joshua Heschel, *The Sabbath*, as quoted in *The
World's Wisdom: Sacred Texts of the World's Religions*,
edited by Philip Novak (New York: HarperOne,
1995).

Abbot Anthony, Amma Syncletica, and Thomas Merton, *The Wisdom of the Desert* (New York: New Directions, 1970).

Fire and Wine

Zuleikha, "Rabia Song," *Robe of Love* (Swan Lake, 2001).

Shefa Gold, personal website, http://rabbishefagold.com.

Works Referenced Throughout

John of the Cross, *Dark Night of the Soul*, translated by Mirabai Starr (New York: Penguin / Riverhead, 2002).

Teresa of Avila, *The Book of My Life*, translated by Mirabai Starr (Boston, MA: Shambhala, 2007).

Teresa of Avila, *The Interior Castle*, translated by Mirabai Starr (New York: Penguin / Riverhead, 2003).

Bibles and Holy Texts

The Essential Koran, translated by Thomas Cleary (San Francisco, CA: HarperSanFrancisco, 1993).

IslamiCity website, http://www.islamicity.com/quransearch.

King James Version

New American Bible

New International Version

New Revised Standard Version

Sublime Quran, revised edition, translated by Laleh Bakhtiar (Chicago: Kazi, 2009).

Tanach, edited by Rabbi Nosson Scherman, Artscroll Series, Stone Edition (Brooklyn, NY: Mesorah, 1996).

RECOMMENDED READING

Armstrong, K. *A History of God*. New York: Ballantine, 1993.

Armstrong, K. *Twelve Steps to a Compassionate Life*. London: Bodley Head, 2011.

Barks, C., trans. *The Essential Rumi*. San Francisco, CA: HarperSanFrancisco, 1995.

Bielecki, T. *Holy Daring: An Outrageous Gift to Modern Spirituality From Saint Teresa, the Grand Wild Woman of Avila*. Rockport, MA: Element, 1994.

Bloch, A., and C. Bloch, trans. *The Song of Songs: A New Translation*. Berkeley, CA: University of California Press, 1995.

Bly, R. *The Winged Energy of Delight: Selected Translations*. New York: HarperPerennial, 2004.

Buber, M. *The Legend of the Baal-Shem*. Princeton, NJ: Princeton University Press, 1955.

Cooper, D. *God Is a Verb: Kabbalah and the Practice of Mystical Judaism*. New York: Riverhead, 1998.

Das, K. *Chants of a Lifetime: Searching for a Heart of Gold*. Carlsbad, CA: Hay House, 2010.

Dass, R., and R. Das. *Be Love Now: The Path of the Heart.* New York: HarperOne, 2010.

Dear, J. *Jesus the Rebel.* London: Sheed & Ward, 2000.

Douglas-Klotz, N. *The Hidden Gospel: Decoding the Spiritual Message of the Aramaic Jesus.* Wheaton, IL: Quest, 1999.

Easwaran, E. *God Makes the Rivers to Flow: Sacred Literature of the World.* Petaluma, CA: Nilgiri, 2003.

Ellsberg, R. *All Saints: Daily Reflections on Saints, Prophets, and Witnesses for our Time.* New York: Crossroads, 2004.

Flinders, C. *Enduring Grace: Living Portraits of Seven Women Mystics.* San Francisco, CA: HarperSanFrancisco, 1993.

Fox, M. *One River, Many Wells.* Los Angeles, CA: Jeremy Tarcher, 2000.

Harvey, A. *The Essential Mystics.* Edison, NJ: Castle, 1996.

Harvey, A. *Teachings of the Christian Mystics.* Boston: Shambhala, 1998.

Helminski, C. *Women of Sufism: A Hidden Treasure.* Boston: Shambhala, 2003.

Heschel, A. *God in Search of Man.* New York: Farrar, Straus and Giroux, 1955.

Heschel, A. *The Prophets.* New York: Harper Torchbooks, 1962.

Hirshfield, J. *Women in Praise of the Sacred: 43 Centuries of Spiritual Poetry by Women.* New York: HarperPerennial, 1994.

Housden, R. *Risking Everything: 110 Poems of Love and Revelation.* New York: Harmony Books, 2003.

Kolin, A., and M. Mafi, trans. *Rumi: Hidden Music.* London: Thorsons, 2001.

Kolin, A., and M. Mafi, trans. *Rumi, Gardens of the Beloved.* Rockport, MA: Element, 2003.

Lerner, M. *Jewish Renewal: A Path to Healing and Transformation.* New York: Grosset / Putnam, 1994.

Martin, J. *My Life With the Saints.* Toronto: Loyola, 2006.

Merton, T. *The Wisdom of the Desert.* New York: New Directions, 1960.

Milosz, C. *A Book of Luminous Things: An International Anthology of Poetry.* Eugene, OR: Harvest, 1996.

Mitchell, S., ed. *The Enlightened Heart: An Anthology of Sacred Poetry.* New York: HarperCollins, 1989.

Mitchell, S., ed. *The Enlightened Mind: An Anthology of Sacred Prose.* New York: HarperCollins, 1989.

Novak, P., ed. *The World's Wisdom: Sacred Texts of the World's Religions.* San Francisco, CA: Harper SanFrancisco, 1994.

Novick, L. *On The Wings of the Shekhinah: Rediscovering Judaism's Divine Feminine.* Wheaton, IL: Quest, 2008.

Pagels, E. *Beyond Belief: The Secret Gospel of Thomas.* New York: Random House, 2003.

Pagels, E. *The Gnostic Gospels.* New York: Vintage, 1989.

Rahman, J. *The Fragrance of Faith, The Enlightened Heart of Islam.* Watsonville, CA: Book Foundation, 2004.

Schachter-Shalomi, Z. *A Heart Afire: Stories and Teachings of the Early Hasidic Masters.* Philadelphia: Jewish Publication Society, 2009.

Shaia, A. *The Hidden Power of the Gospels.* New York: HarperOne, 2010.

Shapiro, R. *The Hebrew Prophets, Selections Annotated & Explained*. Woodstock, VT: Skylight Paths, 2004.

Smith, H. *The World's Religions*. New York: HarperOne, 1991.

Teasdale, W. *The Mystic Heart*. Novato, CA: New World Library, 1999.

Thompson, R. *A Voluptuous God: A Christian Heretic Speaks*. Incline Village, NV: Copper House, 2007.

Von Speyr, A. *The Mission of the Prophets*. San Francisco, CA: Ignatius, 1996.